The
LITTLE BOOK OF ARCHAEOLOGY

Peter Salmon

THE LITTLE BOOK OF ARCHAEOLOGY

An Hachette UK Company
www.hachette.co.uk

Summersdale Publishers
Part of Octopus Publishing Group Limited
Carmelite House
50 Victoria Embankment
LONDON
EC4Y 0DZ
UK

www.summersdale.com

This FSC® label means that materials used for the product have been responsibly sourced

The authorized representative in the EEA is Hachette Ireland, 8 Castlecourt Centre, Castleknock Road, Castleknock, Dublin 15, D15 YF6A, Ireland (email: info@hbgi.ie)

Printed and bound in China

ISBN: 978-1-83799-477-9

Contents

AN INTRODUCTION TO ARCHAEOLOGY

Who are we? Where did we come from? How did those who came before us live? How did they love? How did they make art? Make money? Make communities? What happened when they died? And what can we learn from them about how to live?

Since the human brain reached its present size – around 300,000 years ago! – people have wondered about the world they live in. We have asked questions which, at times, have seemed impossible to answer. We have thought deeply and looked for clues. And a few hundred years ago, we discovered a way of looking at the world that would bring to life the great – and not-so-great – civilizations that came before us.

The Way Was Archaeology

Starting with some of the great adventurers of the eighteenth and nineteenth centuries, archaeology has sought to explore and understand the thousands - possibly millions - of different ways that humans have tackled the great problem of living.

From the first tools to the pyramids and from vast terracotta armies to small jars of oil, everything that falls under the gaze of the archaeologist is a portal to a different world. You will see things that will amaze and astound because they are so different from the things we make, and things that induce the same feeling because they are so similar.

So come along on this fascinating journey - not just into the past, but also into the present and the future. The world will be your oyster - let's open it and have a look inside!

A BEGINNER'S GUIDE TO ARCHAEOLOGY

Have you ever wondered about the people who came before you? Not just the recent ones, but way, way back? That spot where you're sitting – it hasn't always been like that. What was there a hundred years ago? Five hundred? A thousand?

There are times when the human thirst for knowledge becomes overwhelming, not just in individuals but in society, and, in the seventeenth century, it seems you could barely take a step without meeting someone on a quest to discover the past. These people gifted us the vast world of archaeology. But how did it all start? With a man striding towards some rocks...

Archaeology – A New Form of Thinking

Sometime in 1666, a man in a powdered wig and breeches strode across a field carrying a leather-bound notebook and a quill. John Aubrey freely admitted he had a terrible memory, so he was a constant scribbler about things that interested him. The "thing" that interested him on this particular day stood in the middle of a field in Wiltshire, England.

It was called Stonehenge – a stone circle that was already known to be some 5,000 years old, but whose construction and purpose remain mysterious, even today.

Aubrey did not know it but, as he wrote down his impressions of Stonehenge, took measurements, climbed on and around it, and started to think about what the stone circle could be and who the sorts of people were who had built it and lived in its shadow, he was inventing a new form of thinking about the world. It wouldn't be named for another 150 years, but Aubrey was practising what would become known as archaeology – from the Greek words *archaia*, meaning "ancient things", and *logos*, meaning "theory" or "science".

Just the Facts

As we will see as we explore the origins of archaeology, humans have always been fascinated by those who came before them. As far back as 550 BCE, the last king of Mesopotamia, Nabonidus, spent his spare time when not fighting wars digging about in the remains of his Mesopotamian forebears from 2,000 years earlier.

Five hundred to 1,000 years later, Greek and Chinese antiquarians would collect, catalogue and study artefacts from earlier generations. Their interest was to put forward hard facts about the past – not speculations – and that remains a part of archaeology today.

But it was Aubrey who started to think more deeply about how civilizations came into existence and passed away, how they lived, loved, ate and died, and how the things they left behind gave us clues as to their beliefs, hopes and fears.

It was also Aubrey who first wielded an implement that may have even been used by those who built Stonehenge, in much the same form as the one Aubrey came back with soon after: the spade.

Dig It

When most people think of archaeologists, one of two images is likely to come to mind. The first is Indiana Jones, the famous hero of the Steven Spielberg films, with his hat, whip, fear of snakes and love of foiling Nazi plans.

The other, as any archaeologist will tell you, is closer to the truth. Since Aubrey's time, archaeology has mostly been about excavation. Aubrey, with his spade, is the true precursor to the modern archaeologist, realizing that the surface of a site such as Stonehenge could only tell us so much.

If we wanted to know more, we had to dig. We had to, if you like, find out where the bodies were buried. Back in Aubrey's time, there was already a sense that Stonehenge was somehow religious, and whatever gods the people who built it worshipped, it was likely they wanted to be close to their deity when they died.

So, he pulled up his breeches and down he went. And what he came back up with was much more than skulls and bones.

What They Were Doing

As anyone who has watched the film *Spinal Tap* will know, the people Aubrey discovered were the Druids. While the members of *Spinal Tap* famously said, "No one knows who they were or what they were doing," that was exactly the sort of thing John Aubrey *did* want to know.

Aubrey's second major contribution was not just to dig stuff up, but to try and draw conclusions from what he found, which could then help in the calculation of when things were built and by whom. For instance, Aubrey noted that the areas where stone circles were found tended to lack the sort of artefacts associated with communities known to inhabit England in ancient times - the Danes, Romans and Saxons. This led him to conclude that the circles were constructed by native Britons, ancient people from way before Roman times - that is, before 43 CE. In fact, Aubrey put the construction long before that - to the fourth century BCE.

The Stonehenge Archer

Aubrey was not, of course, the last man to tackle the mysteries of Stonehenge. Since his time, hundreds of people have tried to get to the bottom of this mysterious circle.

Nowadays, a date of 3100 BCE is generally given as the start date of construction. Modern archaeological techniques, as we will see, have enabled such things as carbon dating of the rocks to provide more specific information about their age and original location.

Sometimes, however, archaeologists get lucky with old techniques. In 1978, the environmental archaeologist Professor John Evans was looking for snails and accidentally dug up the grave of a young man! That man is now known as the Stonehenge Archer because of the arrows embedded in his body.

No matter the techniques, archaeology still tries to build on the ideas of those like Aubrey, who wanted to know how the people who came before us lived and what we can learn from them and about ourselves.

All Change!

So, it's fine for people like Aubrey to start digging up the past if they want to – but what's in it for us? We live in the now and dream of the future, but what is there to learn from the past? The answer is plenty!

A lot has changed in only the last hundred years, let alone the last 5,000. As someone once said, if one of the great Greek philosophers arrived in the modern world, they would only need to see a train go past to feel like throwing away everything they'd ever written. Imagine if they saw a mobile phone! Even those who were working at NASA in 1969, putting humans on the moon, would be astonished that most of us have more technology in our pocket than the entire system they used – including the spaceship, Apollo 11! (Although perhaps not as astonished as we are that they did what they did with less technology than a Nokia phone!)

Surely, what's past is past. But what can it teach us?

Humanity 101

No matter what has changed around us, in the end, the fundamentals of being a human have remained the same. We breathe, we smile, we cry. We work and play. We seek food and shelter. We make love. Many of us have children. And, of course, we die, and those left behind, hopefully, mourn our passing.

Across cultures and civilizations, these human qualities have not changed. We also tend to have a lot of similar values and dreams. There are regional and chronological variations, of course, but in most places, at most times, it has been wrong to kill. Friendship has been valued as a good thing. Many civilizations have worshipped a god or gods. Wars have been fought; peace deals have been struck.

For over 5,000 years, people have been using money of some kind, exchanging it for goods and services. There have been kings and queens, emperors and empresses, rulers and slaves. Great feats of construction have been undertaken. Small acts of kindness have been carried out, as have big ones - as we shall see.

Off the Page

How do we know this? Well, some of it has been passed down in books and other forms of writing. But books are notoriously fragile things, made of material that decays. They are also particularly partial in what they say. They don't – they *can't* – tell the whole story. For a start, a great many civilizations didn't write things down: some societies had not yet mastered the concept of writing, some lacked the technology, and some were far too busy doing all the work to put pen to paper (those pyramids in Egypt didn't build themselves)! After a long day hoisting stones up a slope, even the most loquacious Egyptian slaves were unlikely to finish their day by taking up the pen.

So we need to look around us, climb up things or dig down.

That way, we can see how people really lived, how they loved, how they worshipped, how they died. We can start to compare how we do things now with how they were done previously, in order not only to learn about them but to learn about ourselves.

Learning About Us

Here's a fun word fact. The word "theory" comes from the ancient Greeks, some 3,000-odd years ago. Their word was *theorin,* which means "to look at", "to observe" or to be "a spectator" - we also get the word "theatre" from a closely related word, meaning "to behold".

So, what were the Greeks looking at, observing, being spectators of or beholding? The answer is other civilizations. The ancient Greek civilization was one of the first literate ones to engage not only in trade with other civilizations but in what we might now call tourism.

As anyone who has ever travelled will know, when you immerse yourself in a new culture, it's the differences that are often so fascinating - different ways of doing things, different etiquette, different styles of dress. Sometimes, it's the small differences that stand out. For example, the people on pedestrian crossing signs might be shorter and stouter in a cold climate than in a hot one - because they're wearing bulky clothes!

But these differences also make you realize that the way you are used to living is just one version of how humans have organized themselves for survival.

What's It For?

Exploring archaeology is like travelling, except you are not only going to a different place but to a different time. And like the ancient Greek tourists, you end up with theories about the civilizations you study and about your own – and yourself! The ancient Sumerians worshipped one way and you worship another – why? This jug is 2,000 years old and has the same shape as the one in your kitchen, but the cups are different – what did they hold? Why is this house built so differently to your own? Why is this one so similar?

Some of the things that archaeologists discover are big things – dwellings, roads, villages, pyramids. These are called *features.* But it is often the smaller things that tell us the most: jewellery, items for cooking, coins, tools, even make-up. These are called *artefacts,* a word that comes from the Latin *arte,* meaning "to use", and *factum,* meaning "something made". Why these things were made, and what they were used for, can tell us a lot about the culture they were a part of...

Anatolian Beauty Secrets

In 2023, archaeologists were excavating a 2,000-year-old marketplace east of the well-preserved Temple of Zeus in Anatolia, Turkey. They were astonished to find cosmetics and jewellery that were thousands of years old. There were ten different colours of blush and eyeshadow, mostly reds and pinks, preserved in their original oyster shells, which served as a similar container as the modern compact.

There were also hundreds of perfume bottles - none of them full, unfortunately - and items of jewellery such as hairpins and necklaces that were used by women. It became obvious that the archaeologists had stumbled upon a shop selling beauty products and that many of the products women used then were very similar to those used today.

Make-up has been part of human civilization for thousands of years: many of our current skincare practices can be traced to the ancient Egyptians; we know that sandalwood and turmeric were used in Indian cosmetics; while books have been written about the changing styles of Chinese eyebrows. And we know the word "cosmetic" comes from *kosmetica*, the ancient Greek word for "harmony" or "serenity".

Product Placement

It is, of course, great to know the habits of Anatolian women, but can these findings give us more insights? The answer is yes! Knowing these sorts of details can also tell us a great deal, not only about this Anatolian culture but about those around it.

For a start, the sort of place that would have such a shop would be reasonably affluent. These expensive items were available to the wider population, not just the rulers. We might also learn something about the relationship between the sexes.

By looking more closely, we might note that some of the ingredients were taken from far away, giving us evidence of trade. By tracing where things came from, we can identify what sort of trade routes were open at the time, which might also give us information about the sort of transport the Anatolians used.

Finally, we might be able to notice similarities between these products and those of other civilizations from the same era. This, too, may point us towards avenues of trade: throughout history, individual cultures have often adopted the styles and fashions of their neighbours, sometimes distant ones.

All this from an oyster shell of blush!

Deep Dive

One of the truly marvellous things about archaeology is that every discovery adds another piece to the puzzle of how a civilization lived. So vast can these bodies of knowledge become that in the twenty-first century, there are more and more types of specialization - so you can choose the type of archaeology that's best for you!

Traditionally, archaeology has been divided into prehistoric - civilizations before the invention of writing - and historic - civilizations after writing was invented. But within these, there are now further subdivisions as the field grows larger and the research technology more specific. We can now explore things in minute detail that only a few years ago seemed destined to be a mystery forever.

As you will see, if your chosen implement ranges from a pickaxe to a microscope, or if you look most fetching in overalls or a wetsuit, then there is a job for you to do in this vast and exciting field. Maybe you could make one of history's great archaeological discoveries, right in your own back garden!

The Prehistoric Archaeologist

The prehistoric archaeologist relies entirely on features and artefacts to build a picture of a culture and a way of life. The focus is on the Stone Age, the Bronze Age and the Iron Age, as these are the times when recognizably human artefacts begin to appear: tools, pottery and decorative items, votive objects (objects for sacred or religious use) as well as the remains of humans and animals.

These three ages are, of course, named for the cutting-edge technology of the time: stone, bronze and iron, so the artefacts are often made of these materials. Great leaps in culture tend to be the result of great leaps in technology – the world has changed dramatically in the hundred years or so since humans invented flight.

Similarly, when bronze was first smelted – when tin and copper were combined – the result was a material much better for weapons and domestic items than stone. Iron was another leap forward. The prehistoric archaeologist can analyze how advanced a society was, and how far it spread, by looking in detail at these objects.

Historic Archaeology

Maybe the greatest leap forward was the advent of writing. People not only lived; they also recorded how they lived – although not always accurately! But they also used writing for another purpose, as do we: admin. Some of the most important pieces for archaeological study are items such as invoices, tax receipts and other evidence of financial transactions. Fun fact: some of the very first pieces of writing discovered are clay tablets from Sumer in the Middle East, dating from 5,000 years ago, and they are business accounts – lists of property, cattle, sheep and wheat for sale. The lesson: keep your receipts!

Of course, a historic archaeologist doesn't just study writing but whole civilizations that existed after writing came along. By combining an analysis of artefacts and features with an analysis of written evidence, we can get an even greater sense of how people lived.

There are always remarkable things to find. When the Dead Sea Scrolls – sacred manuscripts sealed in earthenware jars from the third century BCE to the first century CE – were discovered in 1946, they revealed that the New Testament was only a small part of a huge library of stories. They continue to be studied.

DID YOU KNOW?

One of the greatest discoveries in archaeological history is the Rosetta stone, now housed at the British Museum in London.

Discovered in 1799 in Egypt by a French soldier in Napoleon's army, the stone is part of a larger monument – a fragment, but a big one at over 2 metres tall and nearly 1 metre wide. Written on it are three versions of a decree issued in 196 BCE by King Ptolemy V Epiphanes – mostly telling his people how terrific he was and how lucky they were to have him as their king.

The valuable thing about the Rosetta stone is that the decree is written in three languages: ancient Greek, hieroglyphic Egyptian and demotic Egyptian (the language of the people). Ptolemy obviously wanted every single person in his multicultural kingdom to get the message about his magnificence!

This allowed scholars, who already knew most of the ancient Greek language, to translate the other languages, of which they had much less knowledge. They could also "back translate" to understand Greek words they didn't know.

The term Rosetta stone is now used to refer to the essential clue to any new field of knowledge.

Underwater Archaeology

Do you like water? Then why not become an underwater archaeologist? You get to study materials at the bottom of lakes, rivers and oceans. Anything from small objects discarded by humans to very large ones like the *Titanic*.

All right, we knew the *Titanic* was there, but what of the shipwreck off the coast of the Greek island of Antikythera, discovered in 1901? In the wreckage was what has become known as the Antikythera mechanism, a hand-powered machine for predicting astronomical positions and eclipses decades in advance. This makes it the world's first analogue computer – from the second century BCE!

As well as ships, you might even find an ancient city down there, like Atlit Yam. Discovered off the coast of Israel in 1984 and known to date back to Neolithic times, Atlit Yam features a burial site, a grain store, hundreds of fishhooks and a drystone well. It even has its own stone circle like Stonehenge!

And for something more up-to-date, in 1933, a Royal Air Force commander spotted some ruins underwater as he flew over the mouth of the Nile. Turns out it was the ancient city of Canopus. Statues galore!

Paleopathology

Not so keen on getting wet? Don't worry, there is plenty to do on dry land. Have you considered paleopathology?

This is the study of disease in ancient civilizations, and as you might imagine, learning which ones were susceptible to which diseases, how and where diseases might have spread, and what methods were used to combat them. Ancient medicine is a fascinating area of research in itself.

In addition, by examining bones and teeth, we can understand the diet of a particular civilization, which tells us not only what they ate but how they got their food – farming, fishing, hunting or trade. Fun fact: there are still markers in your bones and intestines that reveal what your mother ate when you were in the womb, even if you are 100 years old – or even if you were 1,000!

So, if you happen to dig up a skeleton, be sure to pass it on to the nearest paleopathologist. They will have a field day.

Environmental Archaeology

One burgeoning field of archaeology is the environmental aspect, which studies the relationship between past societies and the environments they lived in. By studying geological features (geoarchaeology), plant remains (archaeobotany) and animal remains (zooarchaeology), we can see how different societies managed, or failed to manage, the natural world around them.

Were they farmers or hunter-gatherers? Did they have domesticated animals? Were they nomadic? How did the seasons affect them? Many aspects of land use, food production, tool use and occupation patterns can be studied to give greater insight into the ways humans and nature have interacted through the centuries.

This type of archaeology is particularly valued for its relevance to our ongoing relationship with the Earth. What lessons can be learned from past societies about how to create a sustainable environment; in particular, why did some civilizations survive and prosper while others died out? Often, the answer has something to do with the way they lived in their environment and how changes in their world may have led to their survival or demise.

DID YOU KNOW?

You have probably seen pictures of the giant stone heads, called *moai,* on Easter Island (Rapa Nui) in Polynesia. Despite being only 63 square miles, the island is home to over a thousand of these monuments. Some have speculated that it was these monuments that were partly responsible for the extermination of the island's entire population.

Not magic, but ecology. As we have come to understand, natural environments are closely interrelated. We call them ecosystems. When one part of an ecosystem changes, it can have unforeseen effects on everything else.

The moai are very heavy – the biggest one weighs in at 86 tonnes! How did they move them about? Archaeologists have speculated that they used tree trunks to roll them into position. This led to a massive deforestation of the island, changing the ecosystem forever. Not only did it mean they didn't have enough wood left for making boats and fishing, but the new environment was not suited to human life, and the population died out.

Not everyone agrees, but it is an interesting theory. What do you think?

Experimental Archaeologists

Finally, if you don't just want to dig things up and write about them, you might want to consider being an experimental archaeologist. You can have all the theories you like, but sometimes, the only way to understand something is to try using it.

The most famous example is the *Kon-Tiki*, a large raft built by Norwegian explorer Thor Heyerdahl. Archaeologists had been sceptical that people from South America could have reached Polynesia during pre-Columbian (before 1492) times, despite evidence they had been there. It was felt that their boats were just too small and fragile for the journey.

Heyerdahl set out to prove them wrong. He built a raft out of balsa logs and other native materials in the style pre-Columbian civilizations used. Then, with a six-man crew, he set out from Callao, Peru, on the afternoon of 28 April 1947, for the 4,300-mile journey across the Pacific. On 7 August, they arrived on the Tuamotu Islands in Polynesia.

They had made it and proved Heyerdahl right!

Gathering Evidence

So, as you can see, archaeology is a huge and expanding field with lots of opportunities for anyone to get involved. Many archaeologists are professionals, but there is still plenty of room for amateurs. As we will see, some of the greatest archaeological discoveries in history have been made either by accident, like the Rosetta stone, or by amateur sleuths armed with nothing but a spade, a map or maybe a metal detector.

After all, human civilization has been around for thousands of years, and everywhere we step has been stepped on a million more times by people from Neolithic times, the Stone Age, the Bronze Age, the Iron Age, the Industrial Age, right up to now. All it takes is for one of those thousands of people to have dropped something, and you might find one of the great treasures of human existence or something that leads us to understand human history better.

A BRIEF HISTORY OF ARCHAEOLOGY

Archaeology is the study of history through discovered features and artefacts, but it has its own history too: that of brave explorers prepared to go places where they have, sometimes, faced great dangers – even ancient curses!

As they have made their journeys, they have brought back many weird and wonderful discoveries, and every new discovery has been another piece of the puzzle of human life. While the early archaeologists were often individuals on a mission, their work spoke to other explorers, and it still does. Human life is vast – and archaeology keeps finding new ways of making it all fit together.

The Study of the Ancients

As we have seen, the last king of Mesopotamia, Nabonidus, has some claim to being the first archaeologist - the first person we know of who not only dug around but who used what he found to come up with scientific theories about it and the culture it had belonged to. Many in the ancient Greek world also carried out investigations that we might call archaeology. After all, we owe the actual word "archaeology" to them.

But it was not until the nineteenth century that archaeology began to be studied in earnest, when many of the basics of the discipline were systematized by Aubrey and a group of intrepid adventurers whose interest in the past was fired up by some of the discoveries occurring in Egypt.

Their story begins - as many good stories do - with a man chasing a goat.

Tomb Raider

The man in question was a member of the Abd al Rasul family from Luxor, a family known throughout Egypt as grave robbers and tomb raiders. In the mid-eighteenth century, one of his goats ran away. The man set off in pursuit, running up a mountain south of the temple of Queen Hatshepsut. He could hear the goat bleating and realized it had fallen down a shaft. He carefully followed it down and found himself in the largest tomb he had ever seen, filled with mummies, coffins, pottery, paintings and, to his amazement, huge amounts of gold.

The goatherd had discovered the tomb of Ramesses I, the founding pharaoh of ancient Egypt's Nineteenth Dynasty in around 1295 BCE.

To the locals, these tombs, and what was found inside them, had a monetary value far greater than their historical one. The family sold the artefacts to the highest bidders, while keeping their discovery secret. It was only when the market started to be flooded by such objects that suspicions were raised.

The first great age of archaeology had begun.

Facts, Not Theory

Before 1824, when the word archaeologist was mentioned for the first time in the *Oxford English Dictionary*, these explorers were generally known as antiquarians. In both early China and ancient Rome, they would catalogue artefacts from the past, introducing classifications and producing books about them.

There was a small blossoming in the medieval and Renaissance eras, particularly among scholars, and again in the early modern period from 1600–1900, when science as we know it began to emerge, and the call was for evidence rather than faith. When the antiquarian Sir Richard Colt Hoare was called on to describe his method, he said, "We speak from facts, not theory". It was this sort of clarity Aubrey was seeking when he explored Stonehenge.

But after the discovery of the tomb of Ramesses I, it was to Egypt that all eyes turned. If a goat could find a tomb of such spectacular quality, might not people with maps and trowels do even better?

So began a race that would generate almost as many myths as the ancient Egyptians themselves.

The Father of Egyptian Archaeology

In 1861, friends of an eight-year-old boy in Kent, England, were telling him about a Roman villa that had been found on the Isle of Wight. The boy listened in horror as he was told that men were digging it up with shovels. But, he protested, they should be doing it inch by inch, with small trowels and brushes – who knew what little artefacts of value were being destroyed by the rough excavation!

The boy's name was Flinders Petrie, and as he later said of his own personality, he was "already in archaeology by nature". He would grow up to be regarded as the father of Egyptian archaeology.

He started studying British prehistoric monuments and, at 19 years old, produced the most accurate survey of Stonehenge ever attempted. But it was Egypt that called and, still not yet 20, he took himself off to the Great Pyramid of Giza. Although awestruck by them, he was also appalled by the way tombs were being burgled and monuments sold. Egypt was "a house on fire, so rapid was the destruction," he said. He decided he would try to save it.

Changing History

For the next 40 years, Petrie would explore Egypt and the Middle East, and many of his discoveries are among the greatest in archaeological history. During the 1884 excavation of the Temple of Amun in Tanis, Petrie discovered fragments of a colossal statue of Ramses II. He found painted pottery near the Nile, as others had, but produced the first system by which such objects could be dated: by looking at materials, types of glazes and the depth at which they were buried. His book, *Methods and Aims in Archaeology*, was the definitive work of his time and transformed as it took a scientific approach to features and artefacts and gave practical advice on methods of excavation that he had pioneered.

He believed his greatest discovery was the Merneptah Stele – an inscription by Merneptah, a pharaoh in ancient Egypt who reigned from 1213 to 1203 BCE. The text is largely an account of Merneptah's victory over the ancient Libyans, but it contains a word that was believed to be unknown in Egypt at the time: Israel. This changed our knowledge of ancient Egypt, ancient Israel, and the ancient world.

The Apprentice

In 1892, a 17-year-old named Howard Carter turned up at Petrie's excavation site in Amarna, Egypt, looking to learn from the master. Like Petrie, he'd had little formal schooling; also, like Petrie, archaeology was in his blood. A talented artist, he set about copying decorations from tombs, and was seen as a great innovator in this pursuit.

After his time with Petrie, Carter struck out on his own and was appointed Chief Inspector General of Monuments for Upper Egypt, overseeing the systematic explorations around the ancient cities of Thebes and the Valley of the Kings. In the latter, he found the tomb of Thutmose IV, the most magnificent Egyptian tomb of the time. Among the artefacts was a ring bearing the name of ancient Egypt's greatest queen, Hatshepsut.

More discoveries followed, and if these were all Carter achieved, he would still be regarded as one of the greatest archaeologists of all time. But there was one tomb believed to be in the Valley of the Kings that he hadn't yet found. When the First World War came, it seemed he never would. However, once peace was restored, he returned and resumed his search for the tomb of a pharaoh named Tutankhamun.

King Tut

In November 1922, Carter decided to investigate an area he had abandoned a few years before. On 4 November, one of his crew, digging around a stone hut, uncovered a step that was not part of the building. More digging revealed more steps leading down to a doorway, which was stamped with hieroglyphics. Taking extreme care, it wasn't until 26 November that Carter was able to gently prise the door open. His financer, Lord Carnarvon, who had arrived accompanied by his daughter Lady Evelyn Herbert, asked him, "Can you see anything?" Carter replied, "Yes... wonderful things!"

Carter had found the tomb of Tutankhamun, the best preserved and most intact pharaonic tomb ever found.

Carter later wrote, "At first I could see nothing, the hot air escaping from the chamber causing the candle flame to flicker, but presently, as my eyes grew accustomed to the light, details of the room within emerged slowly from the mist, strange animals, statues, and gold - everywhere the glint of gold."

The discovery caused a media frenzy - "Tut-mania" they called it - and songs were written, films made. But something else may have been unleashed...

The Curse of the Mummy

Not long after the discovery of Tutankhamun's tomb, a strange idea took hold of the world. Knowing that tombs were not meant to be disturbed, might not the mummy inside have something to say about it? So began the legend of the curse of the mummy.

Lord Carnarvon, who had paid for Carter's explorations, was the first to experience the curse. Shortly after the tomb was found, he cut open a mosquito bite while shaving. The wound became infected and he died of blood poisoning.

Next up was Carter's pet canary – a cobra entered Carter's house and ate the bird, which until then had been a symbol of good luck. Then the rich US executive George Jay Gould, who had paid to visit the tomb, died of pneumonia, followed by Carnarvon's half-brother Audrey Herbert, who went blind and then died of blood poisoning.

The legend of the curse of the mummy appears in books, films and video games, and it shows no sign of abating to this day. But Carter was firm in his opinion of the phenomenon. "Tommyrot," he called it, before dying, in 1939, of what seem to be natural causes.

DID YOU KNOW?

Egyptian tombs were not built to be viewed by humans; they were built to be viewed by the gods. Many years would be spent building and then preparing tombs, and during their construction, builders performed rituals to ensure that the tomb was pleasing to the supernatural beings on the other side.

There were two essential architectural features: a mortuary chapel above ground so offerings could be made, and the burial chamber where the mummified remains of the dead person would reside, surrounded by the greatest of their earthly goods. This was both a show of prosperity and an offering to the gods. The tombs were also filled with art. Tomb art was sacred and magical and offered a portal between this world and the next – all of it good for tomb raiders and archaeologists.

Tutankhamun was not a particularly important pharaoh – he ascended the throne at the age of nine and was dead by the time he was 18. But no tomb had been as well preserved, nor had a mummy been so intact – when his body was discovered, it was known to be about 3,300 years old!

“Where Are the Trees?”

Tut-mania, and indeed Egypt-mania, swept across the world. While some archaeologists predated or were contemporaries of Petrie and Carter - Switzerland’s Édouard Naville (1844–1926), famed for his work on ancient languages and literature; Germany’s Ludwig Borchardt (1863–1938), who discovered a famous bust of Queen Nefertiti; and Italy’s Giovanni Belzoni (1778–1823), best remembered for his huge physique, which enabled him to carry large statues with ease - it was Tutankhamun’s tomb that made archaeology explode into the public consciousness.

One of the most fascinating Egyptologists was Dorothy Eady. Born in 1904, she was taken to the British Museum by her parents as a young girl, saw a picture of the temple of Pharaoh Seti I, and cried out, “There is my home, but where are the trees?”

For the rest of her life, she believed she was a reincarnated priestess from Seti’s temple and had visions and dreams from that time. She was also said to be fluent in the hieroglyphic language without studying it. Reincarnated or not, she made a huge contribution to Egyptian archaeology until her death in 1981.

A Theory of Everything

But of course, the mania wasn't only restricted to Egypt. With travel becoming easier, eager archaeologists started going further and further afield, to the Middle East and places in Africa. Archaeology was making one of its great leaps forward – along with the developing field of anthropology, which studied *humans*, archaeology was moving towards the idea that their field of study should be all-encompassing.

This shift was down to the work of one man in particular: Augustus Pitt Rivers (1827–1900). He took up archaeology after a long military career, originally collecting military artefacts. But he was not a man to stop collecting, and soon his areas of interest expanded, and they continued to expand. His idea, which would become so influential, was his insistence that all artefacts, not just unique or beautiful ones, should be collected and catalogued. Everyday objects had as much to tell us, if not more, than special ones.

Stratification

Pitt Rivers catalogued his artefacts by type or typologically, and within types by date, or chronologically. To catalogue chronologically, you obviously need to be able to date artefacts properly, and working out ways to do this was part of his genius. He was helped by advances in another field.

While he was doing his work, the field of geology – the study of rocks – was also burgeoning. The nineteenth century produced more and more sophisticated ways of analyzing and dating rocks, including the invention of stratigraphy by the man known as the father of English geology, William Smith (1769–1839).

Studying mine shafts in Somerset, Smith realized that rock layers occurred in a predictable pattern and that the various layers – strata – could always be found in the same positions. By studying the fossils present in the rock – oldest deepest, newest highest – it was possible to tell the age of each layer. Smith's findings influenced both Darwin's theory of evolution and the practice of archaeology itself.

Stratification was first used when the ancient city of Troy (now Hisarlik), in present-day Turkey, was excavated from 1865 onwards. There was not one Troy, but nine, each stacked on top of the other!

Underground Britain

Pitt Rivers' methods were taken up enthusiastically by a great number of archaeologists, most prominently Mortimer Wheeler (1890–1976) and his student, Kathleen Kenyon (1906–1978). The presence of Roman artefacts in Britain drove them, and they both had a great interest in pottery; many of the techniques used in dating and cataloguing ceramics are down to them.

They were also responsible for discovering and excavating many of the great archaeological sites in Britain, from the Iron Age up to the Roman era, helping to stock British museums with some of their most valuable and interesting artefacts.

Kenyon also worked further afield. Her work in Jericho, from 1952 until 1958, made her world-famous. She also excavated in Jerusalem from 1961 to 1967, concentrating on the City of David to the south of Temple Mount. In part, it was her Christianity that led her there – in an age of proof, she wanted to prove there was truth in parts of the Bible.

In addition, she would work with another pioneering woman of twentieth-century archaeology, Gertrude Caton Thompson (1888–1985), on a new site that would make history: Great Zimbabwe.

DID YOU KNOW?

As we have seen, many of the first people to excavate ancient sites were not archaeologists but tomb raiders and grave robbers, who simply sold their finds to the highest bidder. Early archaeologists saw themselves as crusaders, helping to preserve ancient artefacts. For the most part, they did not sell them but donated them to museums.

Recently, this has become a point of controversy. Artefacts from one country, the argument goes, belong to that country as part of its heritage. In fact, in most countries, including Egypt, that is now the law.

But what about things taken in the past, now housed in museums far from where they were discovered?

The lightning rod for this dispute is the Elgin Marbles, housed in the British Museum. These are fifth-century BCE sculptures and other structures taken from the Parthenon in Athens, Greece, between 1801 and 1812 by Lord Elgin (1766–1841) and which the Greek government has argued for many years should be returned. Successive British governments have refused on the grounds that returning artefacts from museums is a “slippery slope” – would museums then be forced to return everything?

Great Zimbabwe

When Caton Thompson and Kenyon arrived at the site of Great Zimbabwe in 1928, a huge controversy was raging in archaeology. Discovered in 1867, Great Zimbabwe was a medieval city, three miles square, believed to have been built in the eleventh century and going to ruin in the fifteenth. It was thought to have been the capital of a kingdom. But whose? Was the city built by Africans or by another civilization?

Most thinkers believed it to be the latter, possibly an Arab or, more specifically, a Middle Eastern people, which had, they believed, ruled over the Africans. At the time, Western Europeans generally tended to divide humanity into "civilized" and "primitive". It was argued that Great Zimbabwe was so sophisticated that primitives could not have built it.

Caton Thompson's work showed that Great Zimbabwe was indeed the work of what she called a "native civilization" - almost certainly the Bantu. For her troubles, she received a great deal of hate mail, which she kept in a file marked "Insane".

When Rhodesia became independent in 1980, it chose a name to honour one of its greatest heritage sites: Zimbabwe.

Before Us

Zimbabwe was not the only place in Africa to attract archaeologists.

In 1933, a scandal rocked Cambridge University. A research fellow, Louis Leakey, married with a newborn child, had just left his wife for a 20-year-old illustrator named Mary Nichol. His funding was cut and he was threatened with expulsion. Undeterred, he took his new partner to the site where he had started working – the Olduvai Gorge in Tanzania. It would turn out to be one of the most important paleoanthropological sites in the world, and Louis and Mary Leakey would, individually and together, come to be regarded as two of the greatest archaeologists in history.

First explored in 1911 by the German archaeologist Wilhem Kattwinkel and found to be a site rich in fossils, it was the Leakeys who were to carry out a series of excavations that would change our understanding of human evolution.

A fossil is the preserved remains of any previously living thing, and there were plenty of human, plant, animal and even microbe fossils at Olduvai. But the thing they found that changed everything was not human bones but "protohuman" ones: our ancestors.

The Cradle of Civilization

As we have seen, archaeology never operates in isolation. Advances in anthropology and geology led to new thinking and techniques, as did evolutionary biology and the ways people thought about cultures, civilizations and race.

Literature also went hand in hand with archaeology. The nineteenth-century Romantic movement, spearheaded by poets like Lord Byron – in 1812, one of the first to protest the removal of the Elgin Marbles – drew inspiration from new discoveries and translations of the Greek poets and dramatists. Greece became the cradle of civilization.

One of the greatest archaeologists of the region was Arthur John Evans. Born in 1851, and an adventurer in his youth, he had settled into a life running the Ashmolean Museum in Oxford until the death of his beloved wife in 1892. Becoming "very restless", as he told friends, he hit the road. His travels took him to Crete, Greece, and specifically Knossos, where his excavations unearthed (a word we get from archaeology) the Palace of Minos. Remarkable in itself – a collection of over 1,000 interlocking rooms forming a religious and administrative centre – the documentation Evans produced was incredibly detailed and set standards still used today.

The Lost City

If the mania for archaeology remained strongest in Britain, the rest of the world was soon catching the disease. German archaeologist Heinrich Schliemann (1822–1890) was hot on the trail of places mentioned in Homer's eighth-century epic poem *The Iliad*, excavating in Troy and Mycenae, Greece. French archaeologist and Catholic Abbé Henri Breuil introduced the 600 astonishing 17,000-year-old cave paintings at Lascaux, France, to the world. In Greece itself, Anna Apostolaki was revolutionizing the field of textiles and embroidery, deepening our understanding of techniques and the importance of certain styles in certain cultures.

North America was soon to catch on, producing one of the twentieth century's greatest archaeologists, Hiram Bingham III (1875–1956). Bingham was one of the first people to investigate Indigenous American heritage, and on a journey to South America in 1908 he discovered the forgotten Inca city of Machu Picchu, the fifteenth-century citadel in Peru. As Caton Thompson had done in Zimbabwe, Bingham revealed the sophistication of Indigenous culture.

Bingham spent the rest of his life investigating the history of the Inca people – his book *Lost City of the Incas* became a bestseller upon its publication in 1948.

"Dear Boy"

It was Mary Leakey who found him. On 17 July 1959, she went to explore one of the Olduvai sites. At about 11 a.m., she noticed part of what she recognized as a skull jutting out just above the ground. The next day, Mary and her team started the delicate process of excavating it.

The skull made headlines around the world. An adolescent male, he was officially named "OH5" (catalogue ID Olduvai Hominin 5). The newspapers dubbed him Nutcracker Man on account of his huge jaw. But Mary named him "Dear Boy". The Leakeys originally believed the skull to be about half a million years old, but research in 1965 revealed it to be from 1.75 million years ago.

Later, after the death of Louis in 1972, Mary would discover other humanoid fossils dating back 3.75 million years. At a place called Laetoli, also in Tanzania, she even found a trail of footprints in volcanic ash dating back 3.7 million years!

The Leakeys were crucial in helping to develop a timeline of human evolution, and Dear Boy is now housed in the Smithsonian.

Back Home

The Leakeys were not alone in their endeavours. One of their team, Kamoya Kimeu, was a Kenyan archaeologist and palaeontologist who would make some of the greatest fossil discoveries in history. Kimeu was also part of a shift in the discipline, from adventurers and scientists *going to* other countries to dig, to people from those actual regions taking charge of their own projects. Two names that stand out are Zahi Hawass and K. C. Chang.

Born near Damietta, Egypt, in 1947, Hawass has been instrumental in giving Egyptology back to the Egyptians, both through his own work and by being a powerful advocate for Egypt's rights to its own antiquities. He and his team have made many discoveries in Giza and are pioneers in the use of CT scans of mummies to analyze how they died - he even scanned our old friend, Tutankhamun, diagnosing malaria!

Born in 1931, K. C. Chang's 1963 *The Archaeology of Ancient China* remains the key book of Chinese antiquities.

Getting Hands Dirty

There have been rapid advances in the last 50 years, and many of the greatest archaeological discoveries have been made in recent times. While the role of solo adventurer has predominantly given way to that of research scientist, archaeology remains a discipline in which one has to get one's hands dirty – literally!

Advances continue to be made in how archaeologists approach their work, and there are always new areas of research and new categories of human endeavour to explore. In the nineteenth century, there were men like John Lubbock (1834–1913), who coined the terms Palaeolithic and Neolithic to separate the "old" and "new" Stone Ages, and more recently, we have Robert John Braidwood (1907–2003), seen as the founder of scientific archaeology, which embraced carbon dating for assessing age.

The history of archaeology is still being written. Many of the changes that will happen in the future will be theoretical, and many will be practical – but all of them will be some combination of the two. As we have seen, new methods and new technologies change the way we do think, and *can* think, about archaeology.

So, what tools have we been using?

METHODS, TOOLS, TECHNIQUES

One of the basic problems of archaeology is, bluntly, getting at the stuff. The things the archaeologist seeks out don't tend to be lying around on the surface of the Earth – they are deep beneath the ground, at the back of caves, underwater or hidden among dense foliage. So, a large part of an archaeologist's job is the battle to, literally, bring hidden things to light.

Over the centuries, ways of doing this have evolved to the point that some archaeologists now point giant lasers from the sky at the Earth to reveal the lost worlds beneath the ground. But, for any archaeologist, some tools will always be the same. Let's start with the basics...

Tools of the Trade

One day, around 2.6 million years ago in the area we now call Ethiopia, a distant ancestor of ours decided that they'd had enough of just tearing at meat or opening shellfish with whatever came to hand. They decided that rather than just grabbing the rock with the sharpest edge, they could use another rock to sharpen the first one. Then they kept that sharper rock and used it again and again.

Our friend had invented tools.

Of course, in a time of socket sets, genetic sequencing and the Large Hadron Collider, a rock sharpener (and indeed a sharp rock) might not seem that great an achievement. But our friend had invented more than that - the advent of tools helped us to move up the food chain and caused our brains to expand more rapidly than any other creature's. Tools turned us into humans.

Some of the first tools of archaeology seem as primitive to us now, compared to current archaeological tools, as those first bits of rock. But, just as nowadays whacking something with a rock still works pretty well, so the first archaeological tools have never quite been put back on the shelf...

The Humble Trowel

One simple rule when dealing with an archaeologist - be they from the seventeenth or the twenty-first century - is don't get between them and their trowel! For as long as people have been trying to dig stuff out of the ground without breaking it, they have been wielding trowels, and some archaeologists are closer to their trowels than they are to other humans. It has to be the right brand, style, handle shape and level of wear; the death of a trowel can be like a death in the family.

The earliest trowels, dating back to the ancient Egyptians and Mesopotamians, were primarily used for plastering walls and floors, as well as for laying bricks and stone. This was the basic trowel. Romans improved the design, making one blade pointy and the other curved - this allowed for the application of mortar around corners and in tight spaces.

It was in the seventeenth century that the tempering of steel made the blades strong enough for digging; just in time for Aubrey to stride towards Stonehenge and get busy.

Basic Kit

The beauty of the trowel is that you can dig in such a way that you are left with complete artefacts, not broken ones – or at least not broken by you! Shovels have their place, but the sound of a pot – or a skull – breaking is never a happy one for an archaeologist (or for anyone, really). Shovels, therefore, are generally used to get down to the layer you wish to carefully excavate.

Once there, as well as trowels, other delicate implements are the staple of an archaeologist's toolkit. Brushes are used to clean away dirt, to clean up the artefacts and to reveal fine details – paintbrushes and even make-up brushes are especially good for this. Archaeologists also use sieves to sift through the soil – it's crucial not to miss anything! In addition, it's useful to have something to blow air to help dislodge soil and sand – some archaeologists swear by turkey basters!

One final thing you'll need for this part of the process is a bucket. You can move dirt; you can move water. And, turned upside down, it magically transforms into a perfectly acceptable chair for when you eat your sandwiches.

For the Record

Of course, digging is only part of the process – you also need to record what you have found. Excavation is a destructive process: archaeological sites are destroyed as they are excavated, so there is only one chance to know what was found on the site and where.

Professional archaeologists carry artefact bags, which they label for their contents to be catalogued and researched later. Therefore, they also need pens, paper (waterproof is best, in case it rains) and labels.

On the label you will want to record a number of details, starting with the size of the site and the artefact, so make sure you have a tape measure. You should also have string to mark out the small piece of territory you are working on, and a compass and spirit level to check the location and the incline – useful knowledge for later.

It is also a good idea to carry a camera and a "photo scale" for reference, as well as a clipboard. And as clever as mobile phones are now, most archaeologists will tell you, at length, why a paper map is best. Try to avoid having this conversation more than once...

The Survey

Speaking of maps – all this assumes that you have made an informed decision to dig at a particular site. Before the first clod of earth is turned, it is vital to perform what is called a survey. The word itself has two meanings: one is what you do in order to decide a location is suitable, while the second is what the results are of that dig.

There are a number of things to consider when deciding if an area is worthy of your attention.

First, is there any history of artefacts being discovered in that area? If so, are they of real archaeological interest? Archaeologists will often turn to literary sources to see if an area is worth examining – not just texts from within the discipline but local histories as well. Oral sources and local knowledge can also be important. Families often pass down stories about particular archaeological features that are no longer there.

Other places lend themselves to exploration because they have been explored in the past, but not thoroughly. As we have seen, until Pitt Rivers, only "precious" objects were deemed worthy of recovering and recording. This leaves large gaps in our knowledge.

Map Regression

Also useful is a method called map regression. By laying maps from different eras in history on top of one another – it is now possible to superimpose them using computers in a process called georeferencing – changes in terrain can be spotted, as can large artefacts (such as dwellings or towers), which were there and are now missing. This sort of field survey enables increasingly accurate information to be gathered without ever visiting a site.

But for the most accurate and comprehensive type of survey, you really have to be there. A huge amount of information can be gathered and processed by an experienced archaeologist just by looking at and identifying artefacts or other archaeological indicators on the surface, often recording aspects of the environment at the time. This fieldwalking, as it is known, remains fundamental to the discipline.

Of course, this only surveys the surface of an area. To go below the surface, it is necessary to undertake what is known as a geophysical survey: digging for information without digging the ground!

Geophysical Surveys

Electrical resistance meters, electromagnetic devices, magnetometers, ground-penetrating radars and the good old metal detector are just some of the tools available today for sub-surface investigations.

Since the 1940s, this sort of equipment has allowed archaeologists to identify metals and other types of material below ground, suggesting the presence of artefacts. This data can be collected and stored at the push of a button.

Nowadays, this sort of surveying can also be done by using aeroplanes or drones, sometimes armed with special cameras or other geophysical equipment. Natural and built features that have disappeared under a layer or layers of soil can be identified.

Aerial archaeology also uses other technology, including radar and lidar (light detection and ranging) imagery, to map an area as landscape features are bounced straight back to the aircraft. This information can be gathered rapidly – archaeologists Arlen and Diane Chase had spent 25 years mapping just nine square miles of the Mayan city of Caracol in Belize, struggling through the dense rainforest. When lidar became available, they spent four days flying above it and mapped 70 square miles!

DID YOU KNOW?

The first metal detector was invented by Alexander Graham Bell, the man who invented the telephone, and it was used to find a bullet inside a US president!

On 2 July 1881, President James Garfield was shot at a railroad station in Washington, D.C. As he lay in hospital, Bell, already famous, was called to his bedside to see if he could help find the bullet.

The device Bell created, while effective, could only scan 2 inches. He adjusted the machine as Garfield groaned, and it scanned deeper – 4 inches this time. But the metal frame of the bed caused interference. When he asked that the president be moved, incredulous doctors drew the line and sent him away. Garfield died two months later of an infection caused by the doctors digging about for the bullet.

The idea was quietly shelved until the 1920s, when two other US inventors, Gerhard Fischer and Shirl Herr, independently came up with their own devices. Herr won the patent and headed off to help Italian dictator Mussolini recover items belonging to the Roman emperor Caligula from the bottom of a lake!

Excavation

Fieldwork and geophysical mapping is called non-intrusive – meaning the area surveyed is not touched, just mapped. An accurate survey of the earthworks and other features such as this means they can be interpreted without the need for excavation. But of course, the type of archaeology that has fired up the human mind for centuries is anything but non-intrusive. It's as intrusive as is humanly possible!

To those outside the field, excavation may seem to be a simple matter. But as we have seen, the practice of archaeology has changed over time, and much of this has to do with the methods and aims of excavation. Where early excavation tended to be simply the crude act of digging until you hit something, since the nineteenth century it has become an increasingly meticulous science.

As the most expensive part of any archaeological mission, it is also the part that needs to be done correctly – an excavation that damages features, artefacts or the environment is, of course, a bad one. But so is one where the exact location of the artefacts discovered is not properly recorded – what is known as the context.

Events, Contexts and Phases

This brings us to the heart of the matter. How does material accumulate? In the language of archaeology, it accumulates in *events.* These may be big - an earthquake, the building of a city, a war - or tiny - a well is built, a tree is planted, a house collapses.

Each event leaves what is called a *context,* which is the primary unit an archaeologist studies. As these events accumulate, they form a sort of layer cake, each one on top of another. This is referred to as the archaeological sequence, and events can be identified as happening at a particular time by where they sit in a particular place. More or less, the higher up, the more recent. Things on the same level are said to be part of the same *phase.*

This knowledge plays a vital role in excavation. During excavation, archaeologists often use stratigraphic excavation to remove phases of the site one layer at a time (phase digging), thus keeping the timeline of the material remains consistent with one another. But it doesn't do so automatically - this information needs to be logged precisely. Errors at this stage can cause huge problems.

Dating Apps

As we know, it was Pitt Rivers who first called for this type of meticulous cataloguing of the process of archaeology. One would imagine he would be delighted by all the advances in technology that have made his own scrupulous records appear imprecise.

For Pitt Rivers, chronology was all-important – not just what an artefact was, but when it was from. That was the value of an object, not its monetary worth.

There are two sorts of dating: relative and absolute. Relative dating is given by the archaeological sequence – this happened first, then this, then this. Phrases such as "earlier than", "later than", and "simultaneous with" are the markers of relative dating.

Absolute dating is much more precise. It attempts to pinpoint a distinct, known interval in time, such as a day, year, century or millennium: this cup is Neolithic; this tree fell in 1587; this roof beam is from 1066.

Throughout history, archaeologists have pursued the dream of precise absolute dating. In Pitt Rivers' day, only historical records and the newly emerging techniques of stratigraphic dating were available. Much has changed!

We Are What We Eat

In 1945, US scientist Wilfred Libby had an interesting thought. A group of scientists had been experimenting with various elements in organic matter that had isotopes with long half-lives. A half-life is the time required for a quantity of a substance to reduce to half of its initial value - from 14 grams down to 7 grams, for instance. The longest they found was radiocarbon-14 (C-14), with a half-life of about 5,730 years.

Libby noted that this isotope existed in all plants and animals - every time we eat, we ingest more C-14, which plants get from the nitrogen in the atmosphere. This means, Libby realized, that when any living thing dies, it still has a store of C-14 inside it. In 5,730 years, it would have half as much. And in another 5,730, half as much again. You could do this calculation around 99 times before the C-14 would be completely gone, which means you can see how much C-14 is in something, going back 50,000 years (by then, about 99.8 per cent of the C-14 will have decayed).

Libby had discovered carbon dating.

Poor Ötzi

The discovery of carbon dating was a seismic event in archaeology – one archaeologist, Frederick Johnson, described it as being like an atomic bomb. Suddenly, a huge number of hypotheses could be tested, and indeed challenged.

Take, for instance, disputes about the ancestral history of Australia's Aboriginal and Torres Strait Islander Peoples. This had long been not just a scientific dispute but a cultural one, involving land rights and traditional owners. Stratification systems had estimated the human colonization of Australia back to a mere 10,000 years, but carbon dating has pushed it back beyond 50,000 years – and new techniques (such as thermoluminescence, which we will come to later) have now pushed it further to around 85,000 years.

Carbon dating has also revolutionized the dating of human bones and bodies. Ötzi, also known as The Iceman, discovered in 1991 in melting ice on the Tyrolean Alps in Austria, was carbon dated and found to have died 5,300 years ago. Poor Ötzi had been shot in the shoulder with an arrow and died in the snow on the mountaintop, preserved at the moment of his death.

Not so good for him, but great for archaeologists.

Seeing the Wood for the Trees

Leonardo da Vinci (1452–1519) had a busy life. When he wasn't painting the *Mona Lisa*, he was inventing helicopters and parachutes and revolutionizing geometry, physics, anatomy, biology, cartography and so on.

He didn't know it, but he was also a pioneer in archaeology – although it would be a few hundred years before the discipline even existed. One day, perhaps to build an automated bobbin winder (he also revolutionized the winding of bobbins), he cut a log in two. As everyone knew, inside the log, there were rings. But what da Vinci realized was that each ring formed annually, and that the thickness of the ring and its colour were determined by the conditions under which the tree grew. The colder the year, the thicker and darker the ring. This is dendrochronology.

So it is possible to date a tree (and whatever the wood is used for later) by the rings – but also to know the weather in particular years, which is useful in exploring a specific phase.

And, as well as being able to date a tree, you can see where it came from – trees from the same region have virtually identical rings!

The Best Thing Before Sliced Bread

New methods of dating features and artefacts continue to be discovered, such as thermoluminescence, which is particularly useful for dating anything that has been burned in the past, as heat changes the "thermoluminescent signature" – how much it glows when measured by a special device.

Why is being able to date burned stuff useful in archaeology? One word: pottery. For thousands of years, humans have been firing objects made of clay into ceramic objects. In fact, pottery may be one of the oldest human inventions – a Venus figurine discovered in Czechia in 1925 has been dated back to 29,000–25,000 BCE! That's 14,000 years before bread was invented.

All these techniques, combined with written records (another absolute way to date something) and relative dating methods, have led to dramatic increases in our ability to know when something happened – an event. And because all archaeology is ultimately intertwined, discovering the date of one event can add to our knowledge about others in the rich tapestry of human history.

And that is even before the biologists come onto the scene...

In Our Genes

When, in 1951, DNA - deoxyribonucleic acid - was deciphered for the first time, there was no doubt that our understanding of what life is changed. As the genetic blueprint of all living things, DNA gives us information about organisms, how they are and how they change, that nothing else can.

In archaeology, it has led to amazing discoveries and spawned a new field: archaeogenetics. By analyzing ancient DNA (now called aDNA), we have genetic evidence of ancient population group migrations, domestication events (when animals became pets, when plants became crops) and plant and animal evolution. In fact, the first fully sequenced ancient human genome was from the permafrosted hair of a man who lived about 4,000 years ago in Greenland.

Archaeogeneticists can now see into the past with astonishing clarity. Not only does it seem that the first human habitation of Africa occurred around 200,000 years ago, but there were only about 1,500 inhabitants!

We also know that about 15,000 years ago, the first dog was domesticated. Whether it was allowed on the furniture, we don't know...

DID YOU KNOW?

One of the most remarkable archaeological discoveries of the twenty-first century took place in a car park in the English city of Leicester. In 1485, King Richard III had been killed in the War of the Roses. A widely hated monarch, he was buried in an unmarked grave and then lost to history.

Rumours had persisted about the location of the grave, and an archaeological excavation of the car park was ordered. On the first day, the skeleton of a man in his thirties was discovered. The man had a curved spine, as Richard was said to have, and had obviously been killed by a sword, which had cut off the back of his skull.

Could this be Richard III?

Carbon dating showed the bones were around the right age, and analysis of his teeth and bones revealed a diet rich in seafood, exotic birds such as swan, crane and heron, and a lot of wine. Food fit for a king!

But it was DNA testing that sealed it – the skeleton's DNA matched that of two of his descendants. The man in the car park was officially confirmed as Richard III. He is now buried in a grave more fitting for a king.

As DNA has given us another window into the past, so have other techniques that examine formerly living things – especially humans. We are now able to use a method called isotype testing to see what a person's diet was and, therefore, the diet of the society around them – or perhaps where they stood in the social hierarchy.

Finally, paleopathology looks at disease as a marker of not just the illness itself, but how the illness spreads and, by extension, patterns of migration. As we learned during the COVID-19 outbreak, infectious disease viruses use humans to carry them around, and if a disease moves from one place to another, we know that humans did too.

These sorts of retrospective diagnoses can not only solve the mystery of an individual death but also why a society – or a plant species – may have died out.

We can't be sure when viruses first arrived on Earth – viruses don't leave fossils – but it is becoming clear that very little, if any, human life predates them. So by exploring them, we explore ourselves – the fundamental task of archaeology.

PREHISTORIC DISCOVERIES

It would be wrong to say that archaeology became simpler when people started to write things down – in many ways, it became more complex – but there is a certain skill in divining the past when all you have to go on is features and artefacts.

For most of the span of human life, the ways in which our distant ancestors lived was a closed book, but in the last few centuries, we have learned things that have not only enriched our knowledge but changed the way we think about ourselves and our future. If our brain likes to ponder the great questions, how did it get that way? And when did it start to do so?

A Boy and His Dog

On 12 September 1940, 18-year-old Marcel Ravidat was walking his dog, Robot, in the village of Montignac in south-western France, when he found a large hole where a tree had been uprooted. The hole went a lot deeper than it first seemed, and Ravidat went to get three of his friends: could this be the legendary secret passage to Lascaux Manor that the local children talked about?

The four boys lit an oil lamp and made their way inside. They soon came to a narrow, 50-foot shaft. Edging their way down, they found themselves in an underground cave. Ravidat held up the torch, and they looked around. What they saw would transform our understanding of human history. It would also transform our understanding of art.

For archaeology, prehistoric times have always held a particular fascination, with two questions at the forefront. How were our prehistoric ancestors different from us? And how were they the same? We know they needed food and shelter, and we know they procreated. We know they died. But the rest? Did they, for instance, make art?

A Nice Little Earner

What the four friends saw, through the dim light of the oil lamp, was walls of paintings. Lots of paintings. It turned out that there were close to 600 of them. Paintings of oxen, horses, stags; paintings of humans, one of whom had the head of a bird. There were also 1,500 carvings and engravings etched into the limestone walls.

The boys did what any boys would have done in the situation: they kept their discovery secret and charged other children a small admission fee to enter. They knew they were on to a nice little earner. But eventually they asked a local historian to come and take a look. Initially sceptical, he too was utterly astonished.

He immediately told the boys to stop anyone coming into the caves to make sure that there was no vandalism or theft. One of the boys, 14-year-old Jacques Marsal, persuaded his parents to let him guard the caves 24/7, and he set up a camp at the entrance. He would go on to be a faithful warden of the Lascaux caves, helping visitors and maintaining the site until his death in 1989.

Michelangelo's Forebears

What the boys, and even the local historian, didn't know - couldn't know - was that they had stumbled upon some of the oldest examples of cave art ever discovered, some 17,000 years old, from the Upper Palaeolithic era. If that were the only value of the Lascaux paintings, it would have been enough.

But their value goes far beyond their age. The paintings are not only old. They are beautiful. They also show a sophisticated grasp of technique that was radical for Renaissance painters of the sixteenth century like Michelangelo, let alone for someone painting 17,000 years ago.

Take the depiction of two bison facing away from each other, in what has become known as the *Hall of Bulls.* Their back legs cross each other - this requires the techniques of perspective and depth of field. The bulls are also foreshortened - they look shorter as they angle towards the viewer - another Renaissance technique. Finally, they have ghost legs, suggesting motion - think cartoons where lines around an image make it look like it is moving.

The prehistoric brain, thought to be a basic instrument back then, obviously had capacities far beyond anyone's wildest dreams.

Zootopia

The Lascaux caves were opened to the public on 14 July 1948, and soon drew 1,200 visitors a day. But exposure to human contact, the heat of visitors' bodies and their carbon dioxide immediately began to damage the paintings. In 1963, the cave was closed, and exact copies of two of the rooms, The Great Hall of the Bulls and The Painted Gallery, were re-created about 200 metres away.

Meanwhile, archaeologists like Abbé Henri Breuil were exploring the historical and artistic significance of the caves. The 600 paintings can be divided into three categories: animals, humans and abstract signs. There are no landscapes. Of the 900 animals, 364 are horses, and there are 90 paintings of stags, plus bison, birds and cattle. There are no images of reindeer, despite us knowing this was the main food source of the time.

The paint is pigment mixed in animal fat. Some sort of swab was used for application, but in some sections, paint has been blown through a tube to create other effects. Intriguingly, the paintings are not all the same age – they are the work of generations.

Shamans?

So, what were the paintings for? One option that has its supporters is that they were for pure aesthetic pleasure. But there seems to be more going on. The absence of reindeer suggests that the animals that are represented had a significance greater than being a food source, which suggests a religious impulse. The human with the bird head suggests a shaman, and one theory is that the paintings were part of a mystical ritual to improve luck in hunting. That the paintings are by many hands over time suggests that this was a community project, while the skill suggests that the role of painter was an elite one.

Perhaps the community would gather before the paintings while a shaman performed rituals to help them on their hunt? The crossed bison seem to be stamping their feet; could the sound of the stamping have been provided by the shaman – or everyone – drumming?

This sort of speculation is what archaeologists do when they are not surveying, digging and discovering. By drawing on knowledge of the time, they try to build a picture of what happened at each new event. And events like those at Lascaux can lead to dramatic reassessments of everything we thought we knew.

Lascaux Practicalities

It is not just on an aesthetic and cultural level that Lascaux provides information for archaeologists – there is also the practical level.

Analysis of the pigments used reveals that not all of them are local. In fact, the nearest source of the manganese oxides the artists used is some 250 kilometres south of Lascaux, in the Pyrenees mountains, on the border with what is now Spain. Did the inhabitants of Lascaux travel those sorts of distances? And was painting so important to them that they would travel that far just to get hold of a particular pigment? Or were there trade routes from the Pyrenees to Lascaux 17,000 years ago? Whichever is the case, it marks a dramatic shift in our understating of Upper Palaeolithic humans, who were not supposed to have such an evolved taste in art, or such sophisticated trading routes.

The Lascaux caves increase our knowledge of prehistoric humans. But they also increase our understanding of how much there is still to learn. It is one of the joys of prehistoric archaeology – we are still discovering things that throw everything up in the air.

DID YOU KNOW?

The Lascaux cave paintings are very old – but they are not the oldest cave paintings ever found. That honour belongs to a group of stencil drawings found in the Cave of Maltravieso in Cáceres, Extremadura, Spain. Do you remember, when you were young, drawing around your hand, maybe even spraying paint on it so a negative image appeared on the paper? These playful artworks, discovered in 1951, have been dated back to 64,000 years ago! This places them in the Middle Palaeolithic era – they were done by Neanderthals.

If you don't think of this as a proper painting, then all you have to do is fast-forward 19,000 years to a cave on the island of Sulawesi in Indonesia, where the oldest known depiction of an animal exists. It is – there is no getting around it – a big, fat pig. A big, fat, warty pig, in fact – warty pigs are a species exclusive to the area, now unfortunately critically endangered. No doubt they were plentiful when this painting was made 45,000 years ago!

The Three Ages – Stone, Bronze and Iron

The paintings at Lascaux belong to the Stone Age. This is one of the three human prehistoric ages first proposed by Scandinavian archaeologist Christian Jürgensen Thomsen in the 1830s: the Stone Age, the Bronze Age and the Iron Age. Thomsen made this division because there was confusion about when artefacts were from, and he wanted to find a way of grouping them. His breakthrough was to explore how they had been cut, and his categories correspond to the main cutting implements of the time.

By definition, prehistoric archaeology cannot rely on written records – it is literally "pre-historic" – so all findings must be based on material evidence, including pottery, burial goods, jewellery and decorative items, human and animal remains such as bones and teeth, as well as cave paintings.

Given the lack of contemporary accounts, prehistoric archaeology is much more open to disputes regarding where something came from, what it did and how that society worked. But this is not a bad thing – quite the opposite! The arguments serve to advance our knowledge and generate new and interesting hypotheses.

The Stone Age

Of the three ages proposed by Thomsen, and adopted by most archaeologists, the Stone Age is not only the most important but the one that has generated the most material and debates. Why is this? There's a very simple reason...

Stretching from around 3.4 million years ago to around 4000 BCE, the Stone Age accounts for a whopping 99.3 per cent of all human history! Whichever way you cut it, and whatever tool you use, that is a lot.

There is some debate as to whether the creature from 3.4 million years ago deserves the name "human" – but *Australopithecus*, with its upright stance and large brain (albeit 35 per cent the size of ours), seems to fit the bill pretty well. The first specimen, the skull of a three-year-old boy, was discovered in South Africa in 1924. Nicknamed the Taung Child for where he was found, it was only by luck that the skull ended up with archaeologists. The workers at a lime works who dug it up gave it to their boss, who gave it to his son, who – thinking it was a monkey – put it on display above his fireplace.

It was only when a friend of the family, archaeology student Josephine Salmons, visited and identified it that the Taung Child became an object of study.

The Piltdown Man Hoax

After Salmons had identified the scull, the Taung Child became an object of study by her mentor, Raymond Dart. It also became the subject of intense debate, with many archaeologists sceptical that the child was in the human line of descent – somewhere between ape and human, as Dart said.

For a start, it was believed at the time that humans first emerged in Asia and not Africa, and that they were 30 million years old, not 3.4 million. But there was another reason for scepticism.

The world of archaeology had not quite recovered from the hoax of Piltdown Man.

Discovered in 1912 in East Sussex, Piltdown Man was presented to the British Geological Society by amateur archaeologist Charles Dawson as the missing link between ape and human.

Initially accepted as genuine, doubts gradually emerged, and Piltdown Man was conclusively exposed as a forgery in 1953 – Dawson had altered the mandible and teeth of an orangutan and combined them with the cranium of a fully developed, small-brained human.

Taung Child was eventually accepted as the first humanoid – our little three-year-old father.

Human Evolution

Throughout the Stone Age, humans continued to evolve. This evolution was not linear, and some stages crossed over, but, broadly, around 2.5 million years ago, the genus *Australopithecus* (Taung Child and friends) became *Homo habilis* (which means "handy man"!). It was around this time that we started using stone tools, and our diets became meat-heavy. There was also a rapid growth in the size of our brain - far beyond what we needed to survive!

Then, 2 million years ago, we became *Homo erectus.* As the name suggests, we were now walking fully upright and were distinguished by our "flat face and prominent nose". We learned to use fire to cook meat and make it tender, which is why our jaws became smaller, as did our teeth. We also became hunter-gatherers, and there is some evidence that there may have been a proto-language - even if it was just saying "Ug" like in caveman cartoons. (Fun fact: when you see a cartoon of a caveman running from a dinosaur, don't forget they lived about 60 million years apart!)

One last stage occurred before getting to us: *Homo neanderthalensis*, better known as Neanderthals.

Family Tree

All these stages of human evolution have generated vast amounts of features and artefacts of archaeological interest, but, for obvious reasons, once we reach the Neanderthals and then *Homo sapiens* (us), our knowledge becomes significantly greater.

There are ongoing disputes about when Neanderthals came into existence – anywhere between 800,000 and 300,000 years ago. For a long time, Neanderthals were represented as stupid – describing someone as a Neanderthal still means this – but as our knowledge has increased, so has our appreciation. Neanderthals could use stone tools, build dwellings, make clothes, treat injuries, use different cooking techniques, make music and – we now think – use speech.

They may have existed simultaneously with *Homo sapiens*, and some genome evidence suggests interbreeding between us and them. So, who knows? Somewhere back in your family tree, there might be a Neanderthal or two; maybe even a chap called Neanderthal 1, whose 40,000-year-old fossils were found in a German cave, the Kleine Feldhofer Grotte, in the Neander Valley – named after Joachim Neander, a seventeenth-century German pastor and hymn-writer, which is where the genus gets its name.

Stone Age Eras

So how do we know all of this about our ancestors, from Taung Child to Neanderthal 1 and beyond? You guessed it: archaeology.

The practice of archaeology has been instrumental in broadening and deepening our understanding of our prehistoric ancestors and, therefore, ourselves. Digging deep, it has come up with ever-more precise names for eras within the Stone Age: from the Palaeolithic (from Greek *palaios*, meaning "old", and *lithos*, meaning "stone") to the Mesolithic (*meso* meaning "middle") and the Neolithic (*neo* meaning "new", as fans of *The Matrix* will know).

Nowadays, archaeologists tend to specialize – particular eras, particular aspects of archaeology – unlike the nineteenth- and early-twentieth-century adventurers who were not especially particular about their searches.

But one of the joys of archaeology is that you sometimes find something that you didn't expect, and suddenly, an expert on Middle Palaeolithic stone tools can find themselves looking at a section of the grand world of archaeology that had never crossed their mind. Such as fish teeth...

Something Fishy

In 2022, a group of archaeologists began surveying a site called Gesher Benot Ya'aqov, located in modern-day Israel. The layer of the site they were exploring was 780,000 years old. As they were digging and clearing, they kept coming across tiny white debris, which turned out to be teeth - fish teeth. And what was remarkable about them was that they were burned.

The site was near Lake Hula. If the archaeologists were right, then the *Homo erectus* communities that lived in the region had been catching fish from the lake, cooking it and eating it - some 600,000 years before we believed humans had done so. As we have seen, eating cooked food was one of the drivers of evolution, so this shift is a seismic one.

One thing, though: the oldest fish hook dates back only 42,000 years, which means that for half a million years, our ancestors fished using their hands to grab them. Perhaps they weren't so bright after all!

But if cooking food can suddenly be pushed back 600,000 years, then what else might be older than we thought?

Stone Tools

Stone tools, that's what.

In 2010, a team led by Shannon McPherron was carrying out a survey in Gona, Ethiopia, when they came across some animal bones, which stratification and DNA testing proved came from about 3.4 million years ago.

What intrigued McPherron and his team was the marks on the bones - they had been inflicted by stone tools. Or, as he cheerfully puts it, "These bones show unambiguous stone-tool cut marks for flesh removal and percussion marks for marrow access."

The discovery extended by 800,000 years the antiquity of stone tools. For many, this meant going back to the drawing board - who knows, perhaps even drawing boards are older than we think! - but it also meant huge opportunities to find other examples.

And so it proved. More evidence of stone tools was subsequently discovered in western China from 2.12 million years ago, which archaeologists believe means there was migration from Africa to Asia way back then, much earlier than previously thought.

All this leads to the question: how did they get there? Perhaps you could be the one to answer it one day?

Smelting Point

When the age of the Vikings came to a close, they must have sensed it. Probably, they gathered together one evening, slapped each other on the back and said, "Hey, good job".

Jack Handey

Ages don't end quite as neatly as comedian Jack Handey put it – it is doubtful that the last humans of the Stone Age knew it was all over. Especially as the moment that changed things may not have seemed all that dramatic.

For many years, we believe, Stone Age people had been trying to make the metal they used for tools and weapons harder. They had copper – some archaeologists even refer to the Copper Age – but copper still didn't really beat whacking someone with a giant rock.

All that changed sometime between 6,000 and 5,000 years BCE – there is evidence of smelting and metallurgy from that time in what is now modern-day Serbia.

To make bronze, you need to take copper and smelt it with tin. Pottery kilns of the time could reach a temperature of 900°C, which was just enough to do the job. Suddenly, whacking someone with a rock was, as we say, old technology.

The Bronze Age

It didn't arrive everywhere at the same time - in some places, such as Russia, there was no Bronze Age, and they went straight from the Stone Age to the Iron Age- but there was a huge shift in what humans could make and, therefore, what humans could do. Tools became harder, stronger and more durable, leading to changes in things like agriculture and homebuilding.

Weapons became more deadly and armour was invented, meaning Bronze Age armies had two advantages. They also lasted a lot longer – a boon for any archaeologist.

But the advent of bronze had other effects. Tin and copper are not necessarily found together, and so trade routes began to develop between civilizations. Some of the oldest Bronze Age artefacts have been found in Iran, suggesting that trading occurred between that civilization and people from what we now call Pakistan and Afghanistan, as well as Mesopotamia (Iraq) and even Tajikistan.

Some archaeologists even call this the first era of globalization – the world had suddenly got smaller. Easy to say if you don't have to ride a camel from Iran to Tajikistan carrying bronze axe heads to sell!

The Sumerians

One day in 1877, French archaeologist Ernest de Sarzec, intrigued by the number of beautiful antiquities appearing in markets around the area, decided to go and explore the lowlands of present-day southern Iraq. Arriving at the small village of Telloh, he began to dig, hoping to find the odd precious artefact of his own.

Instead, he found an entire lost civilization: the Sumerians.

The Sumerians inhabited the Mesopotamia region from around 5300 to 1940 BCE and were one of the greatest civilizations of the Bronze Age – in fact, some call them the creators of modern civilization. They were the first people credited with grand architecture (including pyramids and palaces), and they developed intensive farming methods using irrigation and hydraulic engineering. The first known code of law was theirs, and they were the first to brew beer, which is perhaps why they needed laws!

Sixty seconds to a minute, 60 minutes in an hour – those are Sumerian inventions. And in 1922, a group of four-string instruments, known as the Lyres of Ur, were found, dating back to about 2550 BCE, making them the world's oldest surviving string instruments.

Gilgamesh

The Sumerians may have invented something else: writing. This was, in part, a creation required by trade - business records needed to be kept - and the creation of laws, which needed to be tabulated.

More remarkably, the people who invented writing also seem to have invented literature. In 1850, British archaeologist Austen Henry Layard discovered a vast number of fragments of cuneiform tablets stored away in the Library of Ashurbanipal in Nineveh, in today's Iraq. He took them to the British Museum, and they were translated in 1872. They turned out to be something remarkable, now known as the *Epic of Gilgamesh.* Gilgamesh himself is the prototype for heroes from the Greek epics right up to the present day. Having lost his friend, Enkidu, Gilgamesh takes a long and perilous journey to discover the secret of eternal life, only to be disappointed: "Life, which you look for, you will never find. For when the gods created man, they let death be his share, and life withheld in their own hands."

Is it a religious work or one of literature? Debates continue, and they probably will for thousands of years.

DID YOU KNOW?

Tablet 11 of the *Epic of Gilgamesh* has a story that may seem familiar – a giant flood that lasts six days and nights, after which "all the human beings turned to clay". Our hero is saved – one of the gods told him to build an ark before the rains began! One can imagine the tremendous sense of excitement translator George Smith felt as he translated this passage.

The story of a great flood doesn't only appear in *Gilgamesh* and the Old Testament but also in Hindu texts, Greek mythology, and Mesopotamian and Native American stories.

Was there a giant flood? When and how?

One possibility, of course, is that God or gods did wipe out all of humankind except for a few people in a boat. But archaeologists have put forward other theories. There may have been floods at the end of the Last Glacial Period (115,000–11,700 years ago), which remained in the folk memories of many societies. Or was there a meteor hit, causing giant tsunamis?

We don't know for sure but, as with everything in archaeology, research continues!

The End of Civilization

What happened to the Sumerians? The answer seems to be an odd one: too much salt. Over time, the salinity of the soils in the area led to a gradual – and then rapid – decrease in agricultural yields. Archaeologists have found evidence that the Sumerians did what they could, upgrading irrigation methods and switching from wheat to barley (which is more salt tolerant).

But it was no good. Between 2100 and 1700 BCE, the population decreased by three-fifths. Those that were left packed up and headed north, leaving the land to return to the desert. The great cities of Sumer – including Uruk, with its great temple of Ishtar, discovered by German archaeologist Julius Jordan in 1913 – gradually sank below the very soil that had cost them their civilization. As Gilgamesh had learned, only the gods can live forever.

But the Sumerians had ushered in history in the form of writing, and the prehistoric era was over. But there was one last stage that still needed to play out in many parts of the world: the Iron Age.

The Iron Age

As we have seen, Neolithic kilns had a maximum temperature of about 900°C – perfectly acceptable for bronze but not hot enough to make iron, which needs 1,250°C. As heating and smelting techniques improved, this magical number was reached – but a long time before the Iron Age, which is generally held to have lasted from around 1200 to about 500 BCE.

So why wasn't iron taken up straight away? Well, bronze was still easier and cheaper to make. So why an Iron Age? The answer lies in globalization.

Most of the tin used in smelting bronze was exported around the world from Britain (for instance, from the Scilly Isles) and the Mediterranean. A series of wars cut the trade routes, and metalworkers were forced to seek an alternative to bronze. By the time tin was available again, methods of working in iron had improved to a point where it was now the stronger and cheaper option.

This is more proof that when practising archaeology, you need to look at the whole picture, not just the section you are working on.

Proto-historic

So, the first use of iron and steel happened before the Iron Age – in fact, long before. Japanese archaeologist Hideo Akanuma carried out an analysis of iron fragments found at Kaman-Kalehöyük, Turkey, in 2005, and found that they were from 1800 BCE, about 600 years before the Iron Age.

Further artefacts of similar antiquity have been found in the Ganges Valley in India, and research continues in Africa, where even older artefacts may have been found.

But the true Iron Age beginning in 1200 BCE marks a point where, for those of us living now, the prehistoric becomes the proto-historic or even historic. With Greek literature flourishing from around 800 BCE, the battles our forebears fought with swords and spears – products of the Iron Age – are vividly captured in writing, as given to us by the Sumerians.

The end of the Iron Age is ill-defined – in Western Europe, it tends to be associated with the Roman conquests of the first century BCE, but there was no one moment. For archaeologists, a new era was blossoming – and they were about to start digging for all the Wonders of the Ancient World.

THE ANCIENT WORLD

It started, frankly, with business accounts. However romantically we want to think about the invention of writing and its astonishing capabilities for capturing and changing the world, the initial impetus was to keep track of stuff as societies began to trade with each other and money started to circulate.

But it wasn't long before this strange new human skill began to transform the way we think and the way we live. For archaeologists, untangling the clues of civilizations that reported on themselves became, and remains, an exciting challenge. And didn't those people make some true wonders!

Tears in the Rain

I have gazed on the walls of impregnable Babylon along which chariots may race, and on the Zeus by the banks of the Alpheus, I have seen the hanging gardens, and the Colossus of the Helios, the great man-made mountains of the lofty pyramids, and the gigantic tomb of Mausolus; but when I saw the sacred house of Artemis that towers to the clouds, the others were placed in the shade, for the sun himself has never looked upon its equal outside Olympus.

Antipater of Sidon

For fans of *Blade Runner*, when reading this passage by the poet Antipater from the first century BCE, it is hard not to think of the famous "Tears in the Rain" death scene monologue, improvized by Rutger Hauer as his character dies.

Antipater was the first to name the Seven Wonders of the Ancient World, and six have indeed been lost. But not for want of searching...

The Seven Wonders of the World

The one Wonder that still stands is, of course, the Great Pyramid of Giza in Egypt. We don't need an archaeologist to find it - built in 2560 BCE, it was the world's tallest human-made structure for nearly 4,000 years, until Lincoln Cathedral beat it by 14 metres in 1311.

But three of the Wonders, the Pharos of Alexandria, the Colossus of Rhodes statue, and the Mausoleum of Halicarnassus, were all destroyed by earthquakes. And it was fire that did it for the Temple of Artemis in Ephesus and the Statue of Zeus at Olympia, destroying them in 356 BCE and either 475 CE or 425 CE respectively.

This leaves one more Wonder, which has puzzled and intrigued archaeologists for many years: the Hanging Gardens of Babylon. What exactly were they? Where, exactly, were they? Who created them, and when were they destroyed?

We have moved from prehistory to history, and it is to the literature of the time that archaeologists first turned for clues. Antipater isn't the first writer to mention them, nor is he the last. Can we piece things together to find the gardens?

The Seven Wonders – The Hanging Gardens of Babylon

It was Berossus, the Babylonian priest of the god Marduk, in Mesopotamia, who first mentioned the gardens in 290 BCE. In his telling, they were built by King Nebuchadnezzar II (who ruled 605–562 BCE) for his queen, Amytis, who missed the lush valleys of her homeland in Iran. In another version, the gardens were created by Queen Semiramis (who ruled 824–811 BCE) for reasons unknown.

There is one other possibility: that they never existed in the first place. They are never mentioned in Babylonian texts – could it be they were simply the romantic idea that Greeks had of an eastern garden?

That possibility hasn't discouraged archaeologists from heading off in pursuit of them. Between 1899 and 1917, German archaeologist Robert Koldewey and his 200-strong team unearthed most of Babylon, and a number of Nebuchadnezzar's palaces. While excavating the Southern Citadel, Koldewey discovered a large basement with stone-arch ceilings. Ancient texts showed that only two locations in the city had used stone: part of the Northern Citadel, and the Hanging Gardens. For a long time, it was believed that he had done it...

Sennacherib's Prism

But there was a problem: water. Where Koldewey located the gardens was just too far from the River Euphrates to make it possible to irrigate any garden, let alone one so famously lush. Of course, one of the difficulties with finding a garden over 3,000 years old is that no vegetation remains. But you at least need the possibility there was some.

In 2013, British archaeologist Stephanie Dalley put forward a new theory. Having deciphered Babylonian and Assyrian cuneiform and reinterpreted later Greek and Roman texts, she asserted that the gardens had existed – but that the ancient writers had become confused. The gardens were not in Babylon, but Nineveh, and had been built by King Sennacherib sometime around 700 BCE. Sennacherib himself said they were "a wonder for all people". Dalley's case was supported by cuneiform writing, called Sennacherib's Annals, on what is known as Taylor's Prism, one of three hexagonal prisms discovered by archaeologist Colonel Robert Taylor (1790–1852) in 1830 at Nineveh. It shows Sennacherib's palace complex with a garden featuring trees hanging in the air on terraces and plants suspended on arches.

Dalley is now generally thought to be correct.

The Seven Wonders – The Temple of Artemis

When, in 1858, the magnificently named John Turtle Wood received a commission to design railway stations for the Smyrna-Aidin Railway in Turkey, he found himself becoming increasingly interested in stories about the Temple of Artemis, mentioned in the New Testament but now missing for 500 years.

A true amateur archaeologist, he quit his job at the railway in 1863 and went off in search of the temple. Of how to go about it, he knew nothing - apart from local accounts, he barely knew where to look.

In February 1866, while excavating in the Great Theatre of Ephesus, Wood found some Greek writing, which he understood. It mentioned that statuettes were often carried from the temple to the theatre and back. In a brilliant piece of thinking - the sort that you need to be effective in archaeology - he realized that the statuettes would be heavy, so moving them would need a road.

In 1867, he found one going away from the theatre. It took over two years to clear the road, during which time he had no certainty that his hypothesis was right...

End of the Road

On 31 December 1869, after battles with bandits and earthquakes, Wood got to the end of his road. And there, buried beneath 20 feet of sand, he discovered the Temple of Artemis. It had been built three times in Ephesus, near modern-day Selçuk, and each time with increasing grandeur; it was the third version that was the Wonder.

The second version had been burned down by an arsonist, Herostratus. Alexander the Great, king of Macedonia in 336–323 BCE, offered to rebuild it. But the Ephesians were proud and funded the rebuild themselves. At 115 metres long and 55 metres wide, it was huge. The building included 127 Ionic-style columns and was decorated with fine sculptures and paintings. Among the treasure discovered by Wood was the Ephesian Artemis – a sculpture of a woman with multiple breasts, thought to symbolize fertility. The temple, it seems, was dedicated to her, as well as the goddess of the hunt, Diana.

The Goths destroyed the temple in 268 CE, burning it down. What Wood found was a wreck – but it opened up a whole new vista of archaeology.

The Seven Wonders – Colossus of Rhodes

"Why, man, he doth bestride the narrow world, like a Colossus, and we petty men walk under his huge legs and peep about to find ourselves dishonourable graves."

In William Shakespeare's play *Julius Caesar*, the conspirator Cassius compares Caesar with Colossus, referring to the statue that once stood at the entrance to the Greek island of Rhodes. Erected between 292 and 280 BCE by the sculptor Chares of Lindos, it is said to have stood 33 metres tall. Much like the Statue of Liberty (which is a similar height), it was designed to greet visitors - and to show them the strength of the nation they were approaching.

It only stood for 56 years. In 224 BCE, an earthquake struck Rhodes; the statue broke off at the knees and plummeted into the sea. However, due to its great size and weight, it was not swept away. For the next 800 years, the fallen statue remained what we might call a tourist attraction. Unfortunately, in 653 CE, an Arab force conquered Rhodes, and Colossus was taken apart and sold for scrap!

The Seven Wonders – The Statue of Zeus

The Statue of Zeus at Olympia, another of the Seven Wonders, stood 12 metres tall. Commissioned for an ancient Olympic Games, it was constructed in the Temple of Zeus in the latter half of the fifth century BCE. The geographer Strabo declared that the statue gave the impression that "if Zeus arose and stood erect, he would unroof the temple".

It suffered a similar end as Colossus - felled by an earthquake and its sections looted.

So, if both Colossus and Zeus statues are long gone, what is there for the archaeologist to do? Plenty! For instance, by discovering their locations, we can learn more about the layout of the city they were in and, by extension, similar cities. Also, where and how were they made? Zeus was believed to have been made in the workshop of a sculptor, painter and architect named Phidias. When the studio was rediscovered in 1954 by German archaeologists, they found tools for working gold and ivory, ivory chippings, precious stones and, most exciting of all, terracotta moulds of the type that might have been used for sections of Zeus!

The Seven Wonders – Lighthouse of Alexandria

A lighthouse, yes, but not just any lighthouse. This was the greatest, and every lighthouse since has been based on its design. Standing at over 100 metres tall – one account says 162 metres – it was one of the tallest structures in the world when it was built somewhere between 280 and 247 BCE.

Its base was 118 metres, and it went up in three tapering tiers. At the top was a gigantic mirror – a wonder in itself – which reflected sunlight during the day. At night, a fire was lit.

Four times it was damaged by earthquakes (796, 951, 956, 1303), and four times it survived. In 1353, an earthquake finally destroyed it, with a stub remaining until 1480. Then it suffered the fate of many buildings, which is the bane of archaeologists – its material was used for other buildings.

But not all of it. Since 1994, marine archaeologists have been combing the bottom of the Mediterranean Sea, finding 3,300 pieces of debris, including 60-tonne blocks of granite.

Satellite and sonar imaging of the ocean has also revealed wharves, houses and temples – all victims of the same earthquakes as the great Lighthouse of Alexandria.

The Seven Wonders – Mausoleum at Halicarnassus

The final Wonder, the Mausoleum at Halicarnassus, like the Egyptian tombs, was built to house one man and his family: Mausolus, King of Caria (ruling 377–353 BCE). It is from him that we get the word mausoleum, meaning "above-ground tomb". He didn't live to see construction begin, but his sister – who was also his wife – oversaw the project.

Though it was huge (45 metres tall), its vast size was not the reason it was called a Wonder. That was down to the sheer beauty of its construction and the artworks inside – there were at least 400 sculptures by great artists of the age. Another treasure, since retrieved, was the Jar of Xerxes I, an alabaster jar inscribed by the great Persian king.

Also destroyed by earthquakes, by 1404 only the base was recognizable, and then Crusaders used the stones to build a new castle. It was only in 1852 that British archaeologist Charles Thomas Newton found it again – and, as with the Egyptian tombs, shipped as much back to the British Museum as possible!

Thus, what is left of the final Wonder is now housed in glass cases.

DID YOU KNOW?

In 2001, when a Swiss foundation, New7Wonders, started a campaign to name the Seven New Wonders of the World, one of archaeology's greatest finds – the once-lost city of Machu Picchu – was among the seven chosen by public vote.

The oldest of the other New Wonders is the Great Wall of China, built between the seventh and seventeenth centuries and, as everyone knows, able to be viewed from the moon. Stretching for 21,000 kilometres, it has always been a place of rich archaeological interest – villages and even cities have sprung up and fallen on either side of it as workers followed it across China.

There is also the city of Petra, Jordan, built around 312 BCE. It is one of the world's richest and largest archaeological sites, famous for being cut from red sandstone. The numerous rock-cut tombs reflect architectural influences from the Assyrians through to the Greeks.

With the statue of Christ the Redeemer in Brazil, the Colosseum in Rome, the Taj Mahal in India and the Mayan city of Chichén Itzá in Mexico, we can be sure these Seven Wonders will last forever. Can't we?

The Lost Continent of Atlantis

Of course, once archaeology moves into a period where there is writing, it is not only facts that are recorded but stories and myths as well. As we have seen, archaeologists have been hot on the trail of places mentioned by Greeks such as Homer and Romans such as Virgil since the start of the discipline. The line between fact and fiction is extremely blurred. For every city of Troy found and authenticated, there is a Lost Continent of Atlantis.

First mentioned by the Greek philosopher Plato in a cautionary tale about hubris – that state of excessive pride that leads to a fall – the people of Atlantis once attempted to conquer Athens. When they failed, the gods punished them by submerging all of Atlantis in the Atlantic Ocean (hence its name).

With Plato describing the city as a great naval power, rich in gold and other treasures, unsurprisingly, many great adventurers, pirates, robbers and archaeologists have attempted to find the Lost Continent without any success.

And for many years, no one believed that Atlantis had ever existed...

Theories

Then, in 1882, a man named Ignatius L. Donnelly published *Atlantis: The Antediluvian World.* It was his belief that Atlantis did exist and that it had been destroyed in the Great Flood mentioned in the Bible.

Since then, Atlantis has been a repository for all sorts of myths and ideas – from occultists like the theosophists of the late nineteenth century to the psychic Edgar Cayce, who believed that many people he knew were reincarnated from Atlantis, and that the lost continent would rise again out of the ocean in the 1960s (it didn't).

It was also a favourite spot of the Nazis, who believed a master race had existed on Atlantis and spread across Europe. More recently, theories have been put forward that Atlantis was driven to the bottom of the ocean by a comet, and that archaeologists, in fact, know where it is but won't tell anyone.

Nazca Lines

Sometimes, you need an aeroplane.

In 1940, Paul Kosok, a US historian, was on a flight above Peru to investigate irrigation systems. As he flew over the Nazca Desert, he gazed down at what were known as the Nazca Lines – long, seemingly random, human-made lines extending over an area of around 500 miles. Dug into the earth more than 2,000 years earlier and first mentioned in 1553 in a book about Peruvian culture, they had been assumed to have been trail markers or, Kosok hoped, canals for irrigation.

Then he saw something that stunned him. Some of the lines converged, and made the outline of a bird. There were other plant and animal figures. Later research showed other lines converged on the horizon at the winter solstice in the southern hemisphere. This was no irrigation system.

Kosok spent the rest of his life surveying the lines with the help of archaeologist Richard P. Schaedel. If these weren't roads or canals, then what were they? Why were they built? And how?

Not Just Lines

Research has gradually unlocked the mysteries of the Nazca Lines - but not completely. The how turned out to be quite straightforward - the red topsoil was removed to reveal yellow soil underneath. Widths vary, from 30 centimetres to nearly 2 metres. But the bird that Kosok had seen was just the start of it. As well as hundreds of simple lines and geometric shapes, there are also hundreds of recognizable figures: hummingbirds, fish, condors, monkeys, spiders, lizards, dogs, herons, cats and humans. Some are huge - the hummingbird is 93 metres, as is the monkey; the spider is 47 metres. The condor is an amazing 134 metres. By 2022, 358 of these figures - called geoglyphs - had been identified.

As for their purpose, debates continue, and they seem likely to forever - the civilization that created them is long gone. There seems little doubt that they have a religious significance, but archaeologists have discerned the presence of scientific symbolism - lines that converge on the horizon, constellations, astronomical calendars and signs for places where water is to be found.

One other possibility - perhaps they were just having fun?

DID YOU KNOW?

The geoglyphs – meaning carvings in the earth – at Nazca are part of a long tradition of illustrations on rocks, soils, cliff faces and hills. In archaeological terms, they tend to be large, usually more than 4 metres long. Southern England has many of them, particularly horses and humans.

One of the more mysterious is in Dorset: the Cerne Abbas Giant. Fifty-five metres tall, naked and holding a club, debates have gone on for years about how old it is.

For many years, it was assumed to be very recent in archaeological terms. It is not mentioned in any literature until the seventeenth century. Was it some sort of folly erected to mimic ancient designs? The first mention is, in fact, on 4 November 1694 in a church newsletter, imploring parishioners to donate: "For repairing ye Giant, three shillings."

Then, in 2020, the use of luminescent techniques revealed something that surprised everyone. Samples yielded a date range for construction of 700–1100, around the early medieval or late Anglo-Saxon period.

Which still leaves one mystery: why, for a thousand years, did no one mention a 55-metre man carved into a hillside?

Pompeii

The Nazca Lines were deliberately created, but sometimes an archaeologically important event can happen when it is least expected. The people of the Roman city of Pompeii did live in the shadow of the volcanic Mount Vesuvius, but it had not erupted since 1800 BCE, so they went about their business without giving it much thought.

Then, just after midday on 24 August 79, ash and other debris started raining down on the city. By 25 August, everyone was dead, either swamped in ash or asphyxiated by burning-hot gas.

Seventeen centuries passed.

Then one day in 1738, workers were digging foundations for a summer palace for the king of Naples, Charles VII. The men opened a cavity and were astonished to find other men looking back at them. Dead men. Covered in ash. The people of Pompeii had not just died and been preserved by the ash, they had died and been preserved in the exact position where they lost their lives.

The city of Pompeii had been frozen in time - and would prove to be one of the greatest resources in archaeological history.

Hearth and Home

Pompeii, like any city, had its temples, forums and amphitheatres. But what was remarkable about the site was the preservation of the sorts of things that are normally lost to history – features and artefacts made of perishable materials generally disappear. In Pompeii, they didn't.

So, for the first time, archaeologists had access to small homes, domestic spaces, shops, furniture, paintings. There were bakeries with intact mills, even perfectly preserved loaves of bread. Restaurants and inns, with wine still in bottles, fish sauce on the table and then, as now, open and airy rooms for the wealthy, and smaller and darker rooms, with stools instead of chairs, for the poorer customers. In December 2018, archaeologists discovered the remains of harnessed horses, ready to be ridden.

Surveying of Pompeii has entered its third century – the site has been almost continuously investigated since it was first discovered. This presents problems – Pompeii was preserved because it was protected from the elements and from human contact. For instance, the House of the Gladiators collapsed in 2010 in heavy rainfall due to a lack of proper drainage. Conserving the site has become as important as exploring it.

Terracotta Warriors

Some of the greatest archaeological objects are the funeral sites of the great. One man who obviously worried more about the afterlife than most was Qin Shi Huang, the first emperor of China. Work on his mausoleum began when he became emperor at the age of 13, and 700,000 workers were conscripted for the project. But he felt he needed more than just a fancy tomb. So he built a terracotta army.

We are still not sure how large the army is. Discovered by accident on 29 March 1974 when farmer Yang Zhifa uncovered fragments of pottery, so far 2,000 figures have been found, but it is believed that there are 6,000 more to uncover. Astonishingly, before they were discovered, no one had any idea they existed - they were Qin Shi Huang's secret.

All were painted, all warriors carried real weapons, and no two were alike. And there are not just warriors but also acrobats, strongmen and musicians.

We don't know if they served Qin Shi Huang well in the afterlife. But we do know that together they make up one of the wonders of ancient archaeological history.

Lalibela

If the rock-cut city of Petra is one of the New Seven Wonders of the World, then the rock-cut churches of Lalibela in Ethiopia cannot be far behind in wonder terms. Built in the thirteenth century, the 11 monolithic cave churches were built as a New Jerusalem, hewn from rock. These blocks were further chiselled out, forming doors, windows, columns, floors and roofs. There were also caves and catacombs built for the especially devoted.

One of the churches, Bete Medhane Alem, with its five aisles, is believed to be the largest monolithic church in the world, while Bete Ghiorgis is perhaps the most beautiful with its remarkable cruciform plan. All 11 churches have been places of pilgrimage since they were first carved.

For archaeologists, sometimes the job is to recreate a religion from scant evidence. These churches leave no room for doubt about the devotional practices of a civilization that saw itself as the bulwark of Christianity in Africa, and still does – the churches are used for worship to this day.

The Benin Bronzes

In 1897, British explorer James Phillips, his companions and 200 African porters travelling in the Kingdom of Benin (present-day Nigeria) were killed by the local population. No one knows why – it seems there had been a dispute between the parties, but the cause of it remains a mystery.

The British Empire reacted with fury – they sent troops to avenge the deaths and take artefacts from the kingdom. This was, unequivocally, theft. The troops took 5,000 objects, including figurines, tusks, sculptures of Benin's rulers and an ivory mask. Some were loaned to the British Museum, some were taken by the troops, and others were sold.

The exact location of all the pieces of what are known as the Benin Bronzes is not known – so far, efforts at finding them all have identified objects in 20 countries, held by 131 institutions. Unsurprisingly, Nigeria has asked for them back. Also unsurprisingly, this has been refused.

The Benin Bronzes represent one of the most difficult issues in archaeology. Who owns what?

ARCHAEOLOGY TODAY

From the time of the adventurer archaeologist to the scientifically exact archaeologist of today, some of the basics have clearly remained the same, whether the object being studied is a prehistoric stone tool or an ancient artefact with a well-documented provenance.

But modern archaeology faces new issues that raise ethical questions that never would have occurred to the people who first took up a trowel and started to dig.

This has made things more problematic, but it has also created huge and exciting opportunities, and archaeology seems best suited to tackling them and making them into a new tool in our quest for human understanding.

The Hole in the Shield

On 29 April 1770, Captain James Cook landed at Botany Bay in what would later be named Australia. Cook and his crew were confronted by two members of the local tribe, the Gweagal. No one knows who attacked first – did the Gweagal men throw their spears unprovoked, or did one of Cook's men fire a musket? What is known is that one of the Gweagal was wounded, and the rest of the tribe ran away in terror, leaving their spears and a shield behind. Joseph Banks, Cook's botanist, gathered up about 40 spears and the shield, which had a bullet hole in it.

The first artefacts from Australia had been collected.

Banks brought the shield back to London in 1771 and gave it to his servant, James Roberts. Years later, Roberts sold it to collector John Bowes (1811–1885) for his Bowes Museum.

In 2016, the British Museum lent a shield to the National Museum in Australia for an exhibition, claiming it was the Gweagal shield. Dr Shayne Williams, a Gweagal elder, noted that the shield did not appear to be a design he was familiar with. He asked that investigations begin.

Results published in 2018 established that it was made from red mangrove, which only occurs 500 kilometres north of Botany Bay. It seemed doubtful that it was the original Gweagal shield. But it was still understood to have been from the same era, and thus almost certainly acquired by Cook's men.

A request was made for the shield to be returned, which the British Museum denied. The museum's argument was that it was an important artefact in the history of British and Aboriginal Australia and would not have been preserved if not for the British Museum.

The argument of the Gweagal people was simple: it was their property, and it had huge symbolic meaning for all Indigenous Australians as a remnant of the first encounter with the British, as well as a remnant of their first resistance.

The dispute regarding the shield is ongoing. And what about the spears? Most ended up in Trinity College in Cambridge and, in 1914, were placed in Cambridge University's Museum of Archaeology and Anthropology. However, in March 2023, the museum agreed to return the spears to Australia.

Grave Robbers and Tomb Raiders?

When archaeologists such as Carter began to dig at sites or search for historical treasures, they believed that they were saving artefacts from being pillaged. They thought they were adding the artefacts to the cultural knowledge of humankind - and in many ways, they were. But were they also a type of grave robber and tomb raider?

The question is not just who owns the artefacts, but who owns that cultural knowledge. Despite travelling the world, many of the early archaeologists believed that knowledge was a Western European privilege, and that no matter how glorious the past civilization, no matter how enduring the Indigenous cultures of non-European countries, the greater civilization was the one doing the studying.

It is important to note that a lot of this bias was unconscious - we are all, at times, influenced by what society dictates. It is also important to note that many of those who worked with other cultures were, in fact, at the vanguard of changing attitudes towards the cultures they studied. But the sort of ethical considerations that archaeologists confront now were unthinkable then.

Land Rights

As we have seen, ownership of artefacts is not the only area of controversy in the relationship between archaeology and Aboriginal and Torres Strait Islander Peoples and culture in Australia. The legacy of Australia being designated *terra nullius* – nobody's land – when it was first settled by white Europeans continues to have repercussions, particularly with regard to land rights.

Until the 1950s (back before 1967, when Aboriginal Australians were designated as human in Australian law!), it was often believed that the arrival of the first Aboriginal Peoples had been within the last 10,000 years. This was used to weaken the idea of Aboriginal people having a strong connection to the land.

Archaeologists have gradually revealed how much older that connection is. In the 1960s, low sea levels revealed land bridges linking Australia to Asia, which would have made it accessible during the last Ice Age, over 12,000 years ago. Then carbon darting pushed things back to 40,000 years, while thermoluminescence has pushed it further back to 75,000 years. As DNA testing becomes more common, where might it lead us?

"Primitive" People

Australian Aboriginal Peoples were not the only populations treated as "objects" of study and seen as "primitive". One of the big questions that archaeology has been forced to ask itself is whether the division between "civilized" and "primitive" can be justified in any way.

For a long time, populations and cultures – particularly Indigenous ones – were often compared with earlier versions of civilized humans. Archaeology grew alongside controversial disciplines such as phrenology, which involves observing and feeling a skull to determine an individual's psychological attributes.

Comparing skulls of different ethnic groups was thought to allow for ranking of races, from "least to most evolved" – with no surprises about which societies were deemed to come out on top.

Progress

This brings in the question of progress, which is another that archaeologists must consider. What is "progress"? How do we decide that one civilization is more advanced than another? *Should* we decide?

It is not really a new question. In 1859, as archaeology was in its infancy, Charles Darwin published *On the Origin of Species.* It officially introduced the idea that humans had existed before us, and that they were radically different. Natural selection is the concept that those members of a population that best adapted to specific conditions survived and prospered. This is survival of the fittest - and it applied as much to humans as to other animals.

Darwin was also the first to argue that humans shared a common ancestor with apes - clearly, this was not a popular theory among religious groups.

But archaeology started to make these links. The discovery of Neanderthal 1, three years before *On the Origin of the Species* was published, lent great weight to Darwin's theories.

It was the start of a beautiful friendship between Darwin and archaeology.

Savagery, Barbarism and Civilization

In the 1870s, British social scientist Sir Edward Tylor (1832–1917) began to present human societies in three stages: savagery (hunting and foraging societies), barbarism (simple farming societies) and civilization. As they evolved, civilizations moved from simple to complex.

But how simple were simple societies? One of the great achievements of archaeology has been to show that societies and cultures that seemed simple were, in fact, highly sophisticated – remember the cave paintings at Lascaux? And if Darwin championed adapting to the environment, isn't a civilization that fits its environment and therefore doesn't change dramatically a "better" culture in some way?

The continuity of culture among Aboriginal Australians and Torres Strait Islanders can be read as a strength, or even as a sign of an advanced society. As we shall see, as environmental concerns have become more pronounced in archaeology, a new respect for societies that endure continues to grow.

DID YOU KNOW?

The idea of linear progress in human existence has proven to be an unrealistic theory. Some ancient civilizations are more complex than many of our time. Different civilizations exist at the same time, while similar ones exist at different times. All this is made more complicated by the fact that we are dealing with time frames that are vast. Next time you think it all makes sense, just consider the fact that the great Egyptian queen Cleopatra lived closer to our own time than she did to the building of the pyramids!

And what part does chance play? If a civilization invents something, was it destined to do so? Here's something else to think about. In 1877, Thomas Edison invented the phonograph record using a thin sheet of tinfoil wrapped around a hand-cranked, grooved metal cylinder. In 1889, the metal cylinder was replaced by a wax one. This was the birth of recorded music.

There was no one piece of technology or material that Edison used that was not available to the ancient Egyptians 5,000 years ago...

Slippery Slope

Why have museums consistently resisted efforts to repatriate their holdings? One consideration is what is known as the slippery slope theory. Museums are built on housing objects from cultures and civilizations different to the one where the museum is located – this is why people might like to go and have a look. If every museum had to give back everything it had from another culture, that would be the end of museums, according to this argument. What do you think?

In addition, museums often argue that, rather than acting as cultural vandals, they help cross-cultural exchange – it is through learning about other cultures that we come to appreciate and value them. As we have seen, part of the work of archaeology has been to introduce us to other ways of living, in all their richness and diversity.

Finally, if a museum has the capacity to care for an artefact, does it have a duty to do so? As some have noted, the security of Nigerian museums has been shown to be poor and looting rife. If the Benin Bronzes are returned and then stolen, isn't that a failure of a duty of care?

Moctezuma's Headdress

Another thorny issue is that of restitution and reparation. Since the mid-1980s, multiple groups in Mexico have asked for the return of the last Aztec emperor Moctezuma's feather headdress, taken to Europe in the mid-sixteenth century and currently exhibited in Vienna's Weltmuseum. Made in the sixteenth century, the headdress was restored to its former glory in Vienna in 1878. In 2020, an independent commission representing both Austria and Mexico decided it was too fragile to travel. The people of Mexico continue to ask for it back.

But who would it be given to? The Indigenous community it came from no longer exists, and those Indigenous communities that do exist have not been granted full citizenship. Some have asked the question: is the Mexican government any less oppressive than the colonial powers that took the headdress to begin with? There has also been a demand for reparation - that is, money as a penalty for the initial theft. Would all restitution demands come at this sort of financial cost?

These are incredibly complex questions. And they can involve negotiations at the very top of government.

Mutual Understanding

The rediscovery of Machu Picchu by Bingham in 1911 is one of the greatest moments in the history of archaeology. Bingham excavated thousands of artefacts. The Peruvian government had already passed a law banning historical artefacts from leaving the country, but Bingham convinced them to allow him to take them to Yale University to be studied. The government agreed on the condition that they would be returned the moment they asked. Bingham gave them a written assurance. He died in 1956.

Once the artefacts were at Yale, the university claimed ownership of the collection and insisted that under the laws of the day, finders of antiquities were allowed to keep them. In 2008, the Peruvian government sued for their return; Yale countered that they had waited too long.

Things escalated. The pope got involved, as did then-president Barack Obama. Protesters marched through the streets of Peru. Finally, in 2011, a memorandum of understanding was signed, and the artefacts were returned. The memorandum also sought to set up future relationships between the two parties, including future research opportunities. Could this be the way forward?

Cultural Heritage

Many of these disputes concern historical situations where the parties involved were blind to future implications. Archaeology has recently sought to change its methods so that future work won't suffer the same problems. Sensitivity to cultural heritage is now part of any plan for surveying a site – the effects on the local society and culture of any dig, plus the preservation of features and artefacts in ways that allow them to be studied but which don't compromise their existence.

These impact studies have helped make archaeology a partnership activity between, to use a modern term, stakeholders. The modern archaeologist is no Indiana Jones, shooting sword-wielding locals to get at the treasure. But what is exciting in archaeology today is the same thing as in the days of jimmying open a door to find Tutankhamun: the thrill of seeing something no one has seen before, drawing together two threads of thinking to find a new theory or – and this still happens – making a discovery that changes history!

The Khmer Empire

Where was the biggest empire on Earth in the twelfth century? Don't bother guessing, you won't get it. In 2012, Australian archaeologist Damian Evans got into a helicopter with a lidar device to see through dense undergrowth. He was looking for some cities rumoured to be in a jungle. To his amazement, he didn't just see those couple of cities; he saw more and more. They were spread across 1,901 square kilometres, and some of those cities were vast. In fact, these densely populated cities showed that this had been the world's largest empire in the twelfth century.

He was flying above Cambodia in south-east Asia, and what he was seeing was the Khmer Empire, previously thought of as diminutive compared to others of the time.

The lidar also identified complex water systems hundreds of years before experts thought the technology existed. There are also roads and huge buildings. To the untrained eye, a map of the medieval city below the earth looks like a New York City or a Tokyo, except for the lack of high-rise buildings.

Without lidar technology, this empire may never have been discovered!

The Future of Archaeology

When we look at the future of archaeology, it is to tools like lidar that we turn. This scanner sends 16 laser beams per square metre into the earth, and the time the laser pulse takes to return to the sensor determines the elevation of each individual data point with an accuracy we may as well call exact. It is effective on and under land and water.

Its main use is making high-resolution maps, which it can produce in 3-D. But, as the Cambodia survey shows, it can also be used to find and identify the sorts of objects archaeologists like to uncover, including ancient cities. With lidar, an entire 3-D map of every one of those cities, more or less down to every blade of grass, can be produced and analyzed. In terms of preservation, there is no need to dig up a single part of the complex. Bye-bye, trowel!

Once quantum lidar arrives, these already extremely accurate devices will become even more so. Not just exact, but *really, really* exact.

The Importance of Genetics

It's not just clever devices like lidar that will take archaeology into the future. Advances in DNA and gene technology continue apace - in 2021, the oldest bits of DNA in existence were found in the teeth of a mammoth from 1.2 million years ago. Another mammoth tooth from a similar time has different DNA, meaning it is a different species - so there were two types of mammoth in that part of Siberia. Unless a third, different again, tooth is found...

This DNA can now be sequenced, presenting great opportunities for research and development. No one is entirely sure where our relationship with genetics will take us, and there will be ethical questions to consider, but in archaeology there are huge opportunities for continuing to add to our knowledge of how life has evolved on our planet...

Flying High

Always wanted to be an astronaut? How about an astro-archaeologist? Archaeology has always sought to understand all human endeavour, and the field of space archaeology has begun to open up in response to the volume of human-made objects that now circle our Earth. By analyzing the times and dates of these objects, we can build a picture of a different type of human civilization – one that has its preferences and prejudices like any other.

At least, that is one type of space archaeology, looking up to the stars. There is another: looking down from space at the Earth. Archaeologist Sarah Parcak defines space archaeology as using “any form of air or space-based data” to do archaeology, from Antoine Poidebard – the flying priest who pioneered aerial archaeology in the Middle East, flying over Iraq, Syria and Jordan in the 1920s – to commercial projects such as Google Earth that provide images with increasing resolution.

Parcak’s interest is not just practical. She believes space archaeology has another effect – it allows us “to see a world without borders, full of possibility, past, present and future”.

Everything Everywhere All at Once

This might be the greatest revolution in archaeology of the future, and it is happening now. As we have come to understand the richness of all cultures and moved away from the sort of top-down methods of grading human societies, archaeology has produced a more complicated and holistic version of history. We allow – particularly when it comes to civilizations previously derided as primitive – those civilizations to talk to us in new and interesting ways. New types of sophistication are enabled, not just the conventional ways of seeing that have attempted to measure everything from a particularly Western European point of view. If 99.3 per cent of human history is prehistoric, imagine how little of it is Western European!

Archaeology is letting more and more marginalized voices speak, and perhaps there is no field of human endeavour better suited to this. And yet there is so much more to see. The entry of other social groups into the production of archaeology is perhaps the field's most exciting development in the twenty-first century.

DID YOU KNOW?

Archaeology is a very practical field; but it is also one where theories are conceived and developed, not just about particular places and cultures, but about archaeology itself. There are many intellectual frameworks through which we do archaeology, and these have changed over time, and they will change again.

One change has been from what is known as processual archaeology to post-processual archaeology. The former, which peaked in the 1960s and 70s, argued that we can scientifically study the features and artefacts we find, and use them to develop accurate and objective understandings of the civilization that produced them. Only a lack of information prevents an absolute picture – if we knew everything about a culture, we could understand it perfectly.

Post-processual archaeology disagrees. Developed in the 1970s, it argues that all our judgements about a culture are subjective because we bring our own beliefs and ideas to our study. Every survey is, therefore, an interpretation.

What do you think?

Learning from Those Who Came Before

And if archaeology is to look not only to the past but also to the future, one field that can only be expected to grow is the environmental aspect. Reconstructing past environments and past civilizations' relationships and interactions with the places they inhabited provides archaeologists with insights into how best to reconcile human existence with sustainability.

With the whole of human history as its domain, archaeology can survey how civilizations have survived and prospered, and also how they have declined and died. Sometimes it has been a natural disaster that has ended a civilization, sometimes a disease. Sometimes, as we've seen, it can be as simple as salt in the soil.

Australia has a huge salinity problem. When Western settlers arrived, vast quantities of trees were felled to make pasture for sheep. The water table rose, and now large parts of Australia are no longer arable. This change has happened in just over two hundred years. Aboriginal Australians have 75,000 years of wisdom to bring to the party, and environmental archaeologists can contribute their own experience of agricultural systems to the dialogue.

The Staffordshire Hoard

For all the advances in technology and theory, part of the romance of archaeology is that it can still be done by someone with a trowel, a bucket and a dream. Or perhaps a metal detector.

On 5 July 2009, Terry Herbert was searching an area of recently ploughed farmland in Staffordshire with a metal detector he bought for £2.50 in a car boot sale.

He heard a beep. Well, a series of beeps. Lots and lots of beeps.

He dug into the soil. And he saw an object made of gold. Then another. And another. By the end of the day, he had extracted 244 gold objects. He felt that he'd better tell someone.

Heritage England took over the dig, and the gold kept coming.

Herbert had discovered what has since become known as the Staffordshire Hoard, the largest stash of Anglo-Saxon gold and silver metalwork ever found. There are, so far, 4,600 items of gold and silver and 3,500 items of jewellery, all valued at £3.285 million. One archaeologist described it as "possibly the finest collection of early medieval artefacts ever discovered".

More Hoards to Discover?

The hoard is thought to date from between 650 and 675 and is entirely made up of military artefacts. There are no items of domestic use. This means it was obviously selected and buried for a reason - these are not the remains of a village. It really is buried treasure.

One theory is that the hoard is part of the custom of giving war gear as death duty to the king upon the demise of one of his noblemen. Could this be the property of Peada, briefly king of Mercia in 655-656? It is possible - his reign was short because, according to the history books, he was "very wickedly killed" through his wife's treachery "during the very time of celebrating Easter" in 656. Perhaps he didn't have a chance to go back and collect his loot?

Unsurprisingly, the discovery of the hoard led to a huge upswing in the popularity of metal detecting, and a hit TV comedy, *The Detectorists,* soon followed.

Conclusion

As you have learned, it doesn't take a lot of fancy equipment to be an archaeologist, although if fancy equipment is your bag, go crazy. All you need are a few simple implements and, ideally, a map.

But you do also need another basic thing in any archaeologist's toolkit, from the weekend amateur to the dedicated professional. You need an unquenchable thirst for knowledge. You need to want to know how it is we came to be here, and how people throughout history have tackled life's mysteries. We all only live once, and how we do it is a puzzle we have to learn in the doing – the lessons from the past can help us do it best.

You also need an open mind – to other cultures, other customs, other ways of being. And to the possibility that some of the things you believe about our world are wrong, which is a part of the excitement; it might not just happen that some of the things *you* think turn out to be wrong, but that some of the things that *everyone* thinks turn out to be wrong. You may well end up changing history.

So, what are you waiting for? A trowel and a bucket cost next to nothing. Get out there and dig!

Further Reading

BOOKS

PRACTICAL AND HISTORICAL

Roy and Lesle Adkins, and Victoria Leitch, *The Handbook of British Archaeology* (2008)

Gordon R. Willey and Philip Phillips, *Method and Theory in American Archaeology* (2001)

V. Gordon Childe, *Progress and Archaeology* (1944)

C. W. Seram, *Gods, Graves and Scholars: The Story of Archaeology* (1949)

Mark Smith, *Metal Detecting: A Beginner's Guide* (2014)

Colin Renfrew, *Before Civilization: The Radiocarbon Revolution and Prehistoric Europe* (1990)

Jared Diamond, *Guns, Germs and Steel* (2011)

Steven Mithen, *After the Ice* (2011)

ANCIENT ART

David Lewis-Williams, *The Mind in the Cave: Consciousness and the Origins of Art* (2004)

Jean Clottes, *Return to Chauvet Cave: Excavating the Birthplace of Art* (2003)

MEMOIRS AND BIOGRAPHIES

Howard Carter, *The Tomb of Tutankhamun* (1923)

Agatha Christie, *Come Tell Me How You Live* (1946)

Mary Leakey, *Disclosing the Past* (1984)

Miriam C. Davis, *Dame Kathleen Kenyon: Digging up the Holy Land* (2008)

Julian D. Hayden, *Field Man: Life as a Desert Archaeologist* (2012)

THE FUTURE OF ARCHAEOLOGY

M. Jay Stottman (ed.), *Archaeologists as Activists: Can Archaeologists Change the World?* (2011)

Sarah Parcak, *Archaeology from Space: How the Future Shapes Our Past* (2019)

Sophie Yeo, *Nature's Ghosts: The World We Lost and How to Bring It Back* (2024)

NOVELS ABOUT ARCHAEOLOGY

James A. Michener, *The Source* (1965)

Elizabeth Peters, *Crocodile on the Sandbank: An Amelia Peabody Mystery* (1995)

Wilbur Smith, *The Seventh Scroll* (1995)

Kathleen O'Neal Gear and W. Michael Gear, *The Summoning God* (2000)

Kate Mosse, *Labyrinth* (2005)

FILMS

FEATURE FILMS

Compton Bennett (director), *King Solomon's Mines* (1950)
Mike Newell (director), *The Awakening* (1980)
Steven Spielberg (director), *Raiders of the Lost Ark* (1981)
Stephen Sommers (director), *The Mummy* (1999)
Simon Stone (director), *The Dig* (2021)

DOCUMENTARIES

Thor Heyerdahl (director), *Kon-Tiki* (1950)
Alain Resnais and Chris Marker (directors), *Statues Also Die* (1953)
Patricio Guzmán (director), *Nostalgia for the Light* (2010)
Werner Herzog (director), *Cave of Forgotten Dreams* (2010)
Brent E. Huffman (director), *Saving Mes Aynak* (2014)

WEBSITES

Association for Environmental Archaeology (www.envarch.net)
AWOL: The Ancient World Online
(www.ancientworldonline.blogspot.com)
Current Archaeology (www.archaeology.co.uk)
Friendly Metal Detecting Forum
(www.metaldetectingforum.com)
Trowelblazers – Women in Archaeology
(www.trowelblazers.com)

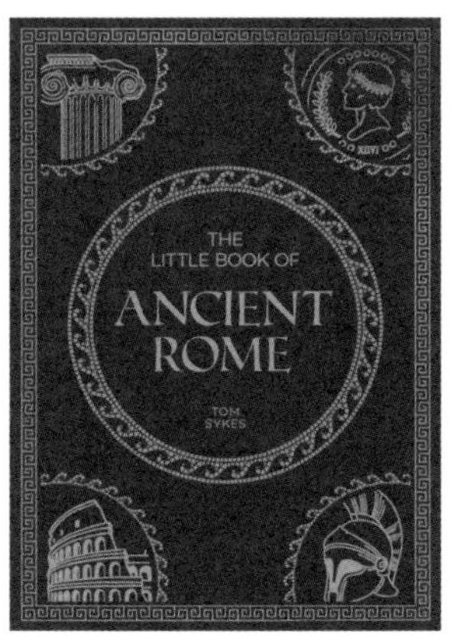

The Little Book of Ancient Rome

Tom Sykes

Paperback • ISBN: 978-1-83799-561-5

Growing from humble origins into a world-spanning empire, the Ancient Roman civilization has captured human imagination for generations. Uncover its history, from the legendary Roman army and its conquests to the art, culture and everyday life of its citizens, in this fascinating little book, which will be your pocket-sized window into the past.

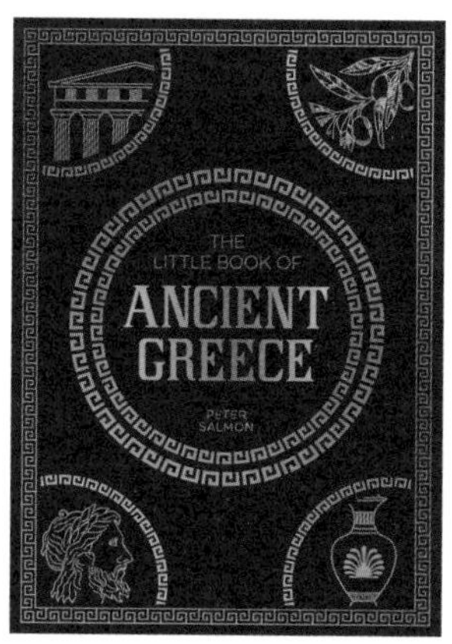

The Little Book of Ancient Greece

Peter Salmon

Paperback • ISBN: 978-1-83799-535-6

If you've ever been curious about the rich culture and vibrant history of Ancient Greece, dive into this whirlwind tour of the highlights of this epic civilization. From warfare and politics to art, culture and everyday life, uncover the key events, people and trivia you need to know to understand this remarkable period of history.

Have you enjoyed this book?
If so, find us on Facebook at **SUMMERSDALE PUBLISHERS**, on Twitter/X at **@SUMMERSDALE** and on Instagram and TikTok at **@SUMMERSDALEBOOKS** and get in touch.
We'd love to hear from you!

WWW.SUMMERSDALE.COM

Image credits

Cover and throughout – archeology icons
© ArnaPhoto/Shutterstock.com